The Tool

*An Inner-active Communication Tool
To Add Balance and Focus
to Your Life*

Larry Hawes PhB
(Participating Human Being)

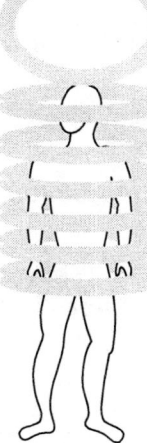

Balance Productions Vista, CA

Copyright © 1997, 2001 by Balance Productions and The Story Teller.
First printing 1997
Second printing 2001 revised.
All rights reserved. No part of this publication may be reproduced, distributed or transmitted in any form or by any means, including photo-copying or recording, or other electronic or mechanical methods, without the prior written permission of the publisher, except in the case of brief quotations embodied in critical reviews and certain other non-commercial uses permitted by copyright law. For permission requests write to the publisher at the address below.

Published by Balance Productions
P.O. Box 1681
Vista, CA 92085
FAX 760 940-8002

Ordering Information:
Individual or quantity of books can be ordered by contacting the above address or the web site @ www.mostwondrous.com.

ISBN 1-878803-06-9

The material presented in The Tool is the author's interpretation of ideas and techniques originally presented by the Story Teller. The actual technique called The Tool is solely owned and copywritten by The Story Teller and Littel Industries.

Printed in the United States of America

Purpose

The purpose of presenting The Tool is to share a method and technique that will allow you the reader the opportunity to incorporate change into your life. In that you will discover a way to consult the greatest friend and teacher you can know — your Self!

Acknowledgments

This is usually the place where an author thanks a list of people without whose participation this book would not be possible. Instead, we'd like to thank *ourselves* for participating in this creative endeavor. We'd like to thank ourselves for:

- The focus and desire to follow a dream;
- Seeing the steps necessary to complete the project;
- Cooperating with ourselves and taking those steps;
- Realizing the tasks that were ours and the tasks that were not;
- Understanding that the project would add to the betterment of all;
- Knowing we had past successes and past failures but they were indeed in the past;
- And for seeing all the possibilities that made it a reality.

Here is a partial list of the people who participated in the creation of this book:

Bix Blankenship	Carolyn Capps	Carol Ghilain	Gwen Jorgenson
MJ Lachowicz	Chuck and Jeri Little	Gwen Manganiello	
Alice Dockendorf	Littel Industries and The Story Teller		

Thank us all very much.

Author's Note

I have always been curious to a fault. I always wondered why the world is the way it is. What was the purpose? Why were we here? Why was I here? I had so many questions. Where was I to find the answers? This curiosity led me to foreign countries and on some wonderful adventures in search of the answers to life's questions.

Throughout that search I always thought a new location or city or job or relationship would get me closer to the answers I was seeking. Then I discovered The Tool. The most powerful thing I found with The Tool was that I didn't need to go anywhere to discover the answers. I didn't need a new job and I didn't need a new lover. *I discovered that the answers I was looking for really do lie within*. I had heard that apparent cliché many times before and my usual response was, "Fine, if the answers are inside me somewhere, how do I find them?"

"Seek and ye shall find," was the next, obvious, cliché answer but the concept never made sense to me and I had no practical way to apply it to my life.

As I learned more about The Tool I discovered it held the key to finding those answers. The Tool offered a step-by-step method to ask the questions that pressed upon my very soul — and get the answers I could actually use! Although The Tool didn't immediately give the perfect answers to all of my questions *it did teach me which questions were worth asking, and that the answers I discovered were worth listening to.*

In the beginning the Tool was not the friend and help that it is today. It was not easy to start, and not easy to understand. It took awhile before I was able to see the magic of the process. I don't know if The Tool can ever truly be mastered. It does, however, offer a method of introspection that will uncover practical answers to life's everyday problems and stresses.

The Tool seems to unfold and develop into so many different forms. Ten years ago I began with the fairly rigid forms presented in this book and then developed a way that works best for me.

After becoming acquainted with the Tool, it now has become second nature in my life and it is hard to imagine living without it.

Is my life perfect? Hardly. Do I still hide my fears and deny some pieces of me from me? Of course, because I am human. But I want to know more, and I want to know more about me. The Tool offers a way to learn all that I desire.

I am amazed by how much I have discovered and learned about myself through the Tool. It seems that *the learning never ends*. That concept might have seemed frightening to me at some time in my life, but now I find it the most exciting thought I could have. The learning indeed does not end.

I invite you to begin by joining me on a great journey of discovery. One that does not require the kind of courage it takes to fight lions or to bungie jump from the highest bridge. This journey requires much more. It is a journey inward, to face the greatest challenges and to discover the greatest friend you could ever hope to find: You!!

What's a PhB and How Do You Get One?

This honorary title was born out of a frustration I felt when I realized that most self help books had the letters PhD after the author's name. I thought it was a great title for the people who had made the sacrifices necessary to achieve it, but I found that the truths the so-called experts would present as absolute fact did not necessarily pertain to my life. It appeared that indeed they had found answers to some of life's questions but I soon realized they were *their* answers to *their* questions.

What was I to do? I had questions too, but they were my questions and they needed my answers. As I became more proficient with the Tool I began to see that I really did have all the questions, and all of the answers that pertained to my life, within me. This realization and growing ability, I thought, should have a title of some sort as well, hence PhB.

The letters stand for Participating Human Being and you get one by being one. Being a PhB entails learning skills of self-discovery. The first is the ability and willingness to become involved in your own life. Next, begin to ask yourself the questions that are important to you, start to trust the answers to those questions and take steps that are true to those answers.

You will see your life change and your new attitude can begin to create the world you want to see instead of the one you dread.

The title of PhB is not bestowed by some benevolent entity that has determined you deserve the title. Instead it is given to you, by you, and you are the only one who can determine when you have become one. There is, alas, no course you can take; (unless you want to call life a course) it is simply an honorary title you give to yourself.

The Tool offers one of the best ways to know all you choose to know about yourself, and for yourself. This self-knowledge can allow you to embrace many of the old fears that drive your life. It can show you the truth, and the truth can lead to the participation that we all desire in our lives. The participation, of course, qualifies you as a PhB.

Go for it!

The Tool

Introduction

We all seem to have them. Those internal, emotional parts of us that drive us to react to situations in ways that are inappropriate. We yell at the kids. We clam up when 'that' subject arises. We retreat in fear instead of acting in ways that help ourselves and others. You might know the feeling when your mother says that one thing and — Gotcha! The gut tightens, the adrenaline pumps, and the words start flying out of your mouth. Only later do you get the chance to wonder, "Damn, I wish I knew why I react the way I do when she says those things."

These internal, reactive spots are often called buttons or sore spots. Whatever name we give them, there seems to be some emotional piece of us that lies hidden and unresolved, a piece that drives our actions and reactions in our lives.

Is anyone immune? Does anyone *not* have buttons? I don't know the answer to that question, but I know I have them, and I know lots of other people who have them, and I know lots of other people who have them as well. Some of us have gotten very good at hiding our buttons from ourselves. Unfortunately, it seems they are a thing that we cannot hide for long. They always surface in some form. If not in anger or frustration or anxiety, then they wait and show up in some sort of disease or illness.

So what's wrong with buttons? Nothing, as long as you recognize that you have them, and that you are able to find a method where *you* are driving your life, not your buttons.

If you find that your buttons are driving your life in a way that is paralyzing or just plain painful, and you want to change that, the Tool is written for you.

The Tool talks about 'chakras' and 'energies' and delves into some very different concepts about life. These concepts might seem a little strange if you are not familiar with them but they are worth understanding, even if you have never heard of a chakra.

You do not have to qualify to use the Tool with years of chanting or meditating under bodhi trees. It is meant for everyone to use.

Absolutely No Absolutes

The information in this book is not meant to be presented as absolute fact. The ideas and concepts are based solely on the perceptions of the author and many cannot be proven by scientific means. They can be proven, however, in your life. If the ideas make sense to you in your life, consider them true; if they don't make sense, consider them untrue.

Unfinished Work

The Tool is a book that is unique in that it can never truly be a finished work. It can't be finished because, as each person uses it, another chapter is added and it changes to reflect the character of that person. It grows and becomes as unique as the person using it. For this reason we have added a section in the back that you can use as a personal journal.

This journal is designed to allow you a place where you can be entirely truthful with yourself. Not a place to hide things from the rest of the world, but a place to record the secrets you alone know about yourself.

A place where you can record the truth of your fears and the things that cause you to react. A place to say, "Yes this makes me crazy, and I haven't found a way to change it."

This book is unfinished in another regard as well. I, as the author, simply have more to say. As I spend time within my life and with the help of The Tool there are many more discoveries to be made and shared with the readers. Those discoveries will be shared in future editions, but for now please enjoy what is presented in this first edition.

Is The Tool For Real?

So how will you know if the Tool is for real? The Tool is for real if it makes sense to you, and if it works in your life. The Tool is for real if it adds a balance and order to your life that was not there before. Simple.

Remember, if a rock speaks the truth .... listen. In the same way, if the Tool works, use it. If it doesn't, don't. (This is the *only* absolute.)

Part 1

The Tool

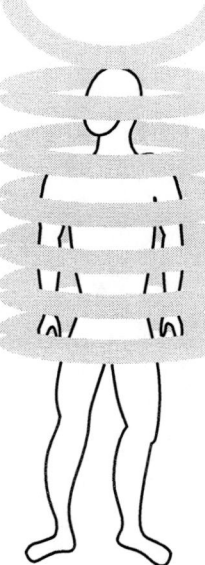

The Tool

What is The Tool?

The Tool is a seven step method of personal contemplation. It offers a way to talk and consult with your 'self' in order to become your own best counselor and advisor, to answer questions, resolve issues, and relieve stress in your life.

It is hoped that the Tool will help uncover the magical being within each one of us and to enable us to create with the most joy and pleasure, and experience our greatest expansion as human beings.

This is done by uncovering and dealing with the invisible, protective veil that shields us from reaching our potential—our fears. The Tool presents a method that shows how we can address our fears in a way that is participatory rather than reactionary. Mostly though, the Tool is about *not* being controlled by the past.

The Tool

Our past experiences are a very useful part of who we are as they lend a foundation for us to stand on and create from. We are able to recognize every part of our world that is useful because of our past experience. We know where to get food, how to drive a car etc., all based on the past.

Our past, however, also includes the fear and pain we felt as children. All of those times when we perceived that we were abandoned or ignored are also part of the past. Those childhood fears, if left unresolved, can be very powerful creative forces in our adult lives. Without a way to examine them and perceive them in a more appropriate, clear manner, they can begin to control our lives in ways that are most undesirable. Like any other part of the past, these childhood fears are not to be ignored, for they also serve a valuable purpose in our lives, but it is best if they can be placed in their proper perspective. They truly are more relevant and appropriate to the past.

The Tool gives us a way to examine these past experiences through different eyes. These different eyes won't change the events of the past, but they *will* change the way those events are perceived. The Tool is a method that can present a larger perspective of the events of our life and this new perception can allow for a more appropriate view of *all* our experiences.

The Tool is not the only way to discover the truth about yourself, but it is one of the most gentle, consistent methods that you can always count on. After learning this process, you will have a tool and a friend that you can confide in for the rest of your life.

Change, Change, Change

The Tool is also about change. It creates a platform for change—it changes as you change—it evolves and moves and can be nailed down only long enough to be experienced, then it moves again. As with Life, change is an integral part of the Tool.

Within these pages you will find questions and answers and suggested ways to use the Tool. It should be remembered that as you read the questions and answers it is the *intention* of the question that is the key, *not* the concrete form of the question. We'll go into this in more detail in the section entitled 'Using The Tool.'

The Tool

The Tool gives us a way to examine these past experiences through different eyes.

Don't worry about the details for now, just think a little about change. How does it affect you? Do you like it? Does all this talk of change scare you a little? Does it excite you? Whatever your reaction to change, the first question to ask yourself when considering The Tool, "Do I want to change some aspect of who I am?" If the answer is yes, The Tool will allow you to incorporate that change into your life in a way that is gentle and participatory. And what if you don't want to change? No big deal. You can still use the Tool to find out who you are, then change only what you choose.

Not for The Quiet Mind

The Tool is not a meditation technique for simply quieting the mind. A quiet mind has a beneficial effect on the physical body but little effect on the other parts of our life. To quiet the mind might remove a person from life in a way that is counter to the purpose of our being here. We are here to create and to participate with life, not to escape from it.

Works Almost Anywhere

While the technique for the Tool is shown as a form of inward contemplation done while quiet and lying down, it can also be done when walking, jogging, or in the shower.

The Tool also works great when recorded in written form. For some people, writing down their experiences with the Tool can be the easiest and the most productive method. For this reason we have included the workbook previously mentioned, to help guide you through the process. Find what works for you, but first try the methods described to get the feel of the process and to lessen any distractions that might occur.

It Might Not Be Easy

The Tool is not necessarily easy to use, and the results might not be exactly as you expect them to be; however, if you use it and learn to be impeccable with what you observe about yourself, it will change your life for the better.

Will you be happy with what you find? Maybe not at first, but if you keep using The Tool, the protective layers of fear and untruths that we can wrap around our world will begin to unfold and the pain you might have felt in a given situation will begin to fade. Fear and frustration will not find a way to control your life, and the excited, creative being that you are will emerge.

Impeccability

"Impeccable" is an important word to consider when dealing with the Tool. Simply put, to be impeccable is *to acknowledge, to yourself, the truth of the different aspects of who you are and decide whether or not you want to change them.*

The Tool is used to ask questions of yourself. The answers you receive will be answers *from* you, *to* you. Are you able to hear the truth of who you are? It's not easy sometimes. Again, it requires that you be *impeccable* with yourself and perhaps that you look at things in a different light than you are used to.

When you find any parts of yourself that you didn't know were there, you don't have to make a big deal out of it. Just recognize the truth of those pieces *to yourself.* That's impeccable. There's nothing wrong with knowing you are judgmental, or jealous, or opinionated, or whatever. As long as you *know it,* then you will have a chance to change it—if you want to.

> *We have learned to deny who we are, and then seek to blame others for the way we are, the way we feel, or the way our life is.*

Sounds simple but we have not learned to be impeccable in our society. We have learned to deny who we are, and then seek to blame others for the way we are, the way we feel, or the way our life is. We then set up an internal conflict that is hard to resolve. Imagine what happens internally when a feeling like jealousy arises and we claim, "I'm not jealous." Or we stuff the feeling because it is uncomfortable. Stuffing is just another form of denial. Simply denying the truth of who you are can be very painful and totally unnecessary.

I was a master stuffer. I don't remember a true emotional feeling until I was almost 30 years old. I didn't know what they were, I wouldn't admit I had them, and if I ignored the inkling of a feeling long enough it would seem to go away.

I then had a couple of traumatic deaths in my life that caused me to feel again. Profound and very deep sorrow and other emotions that had built up my entire life. When I started feeling I didn't think I would ever stop. I would cry at 'Little House on the Prairie' when the barn burned down for the fourth time. I would cry at a sunrise or a sunset, it didn't matter. I thought I was an emotional wreck. The truth was I was becoming an emotional being.

It was suddenly not only OK to feel again, but these new-found emotions became the only real evidence I had of being alive. My physical reality was still important, but now I had a new reality that was just as valid—my emotional reality.

The Tool helped me learn that it was all right to say, "Wait, I *am* jealous, and I like it just fine," or "I'm jealous and I want to change that aspect of who I am."

The Tool helped me realize so many parts of me that I had long ago hidden. Uncovering them has not been easy, but the relief of just knowing and acknowledging the truth of who I am is one of the greatest gifts I have ever given myself.

So remember, as you get more familiar with this process you might hear that little voice inside you saying, "You are reacting this way because there is a fear of _____." Listen closely, trust what you hear, be impeccable and don't throw the answer away. It is *you* trying to be truthful with *you*.

The Tool

When you find yourself in an argument that is blazing fast and furious, it might be wise to take a deep breath, stop for a moment and say to yourself, "Wait, what am I *really* feeling here?" You might hear you are frightened of being abandoned, or of being controlled or any number of other fears. Whatever you hear is you, being truthful and impeccable with you. Listen. It allows you to address what is really going on in the situation.

Being impeccable doesn't mean that you have to be totally truthful in every regard with every person you meet and talk to. Impeccability only means to begin to listen to the truth of who you are and what you are feeling.

If you think you must be totally honest in every situation, first consider if your version of 'the truth' harms another or helps. If you can see that 'the truth' will harm the relationship, control your self and leave those parts to yourself. I did not say lie or deceive, I am only suggesting that 'truth' may be a subjective commodity and how you use it can be beneficial or harmful. It's your choice.

If you think you must be totally honest in every situation, first consider if your version of 'the truth' harms another or helps.

The Tool

Once you learn that the truth of who you are merely adds to your knowledge of yourself, you may want to find out more. The Tool offers a wonderful way to discover these mysteries and become impeccable with your own best guide and teacher—*yourself*.

Fear

As this book began to take shape I was really surprised at how much it began to speak about fear. I read and re-read the text and kept coming up with this relationship between fear and our ability to enjoy life. Fear is so key to our nature as humans it became an entire section of the book and, in my mind one of the fundamental keys to understanding ourselves as human beings.

I think we forget about our animal nature and the roots from which we sprang. It is my opinion that fear drives us in more ways than we can imagine and to ignore that basic nature is to ignore the very foundation of the human animal.

This section of the book is intended to explore that nature and to hopefully shed some light on the complex relationship between fear and the way we either act with, or react to, life.

We begin with fear and what it represents. Fear is basically the phenomenon that pumps adrenaline through our bodies when we sense danger. It really is that simple, yet the way it manifests itself in each of us and within our society is quite complex.

What begins as fear can grow, if ignored long enough, into anger. Anger ignored long enough can grow into hate. As we begin to explore the nature of fear these relationships will, hopefully, become more clear and easier to understand and it is these fears and angers that The Tool will address.

We all have some sense of the feelings I just referred to. It is simply those times that we feel emotionally uncomfortable. This uncomfortable feeling can range from mild discomfort to outright rage. The Tool is designed to discover and address the truth of those feelings so they can be changed.

Fear and Anger

Though fear is at the root of most internal conflict, many of the issues that surface while using The Tool will begin as anger. Anger comes in two varieties. One type is based in what can be termed as righteous indignation. As an example, when an agreement that you made with someone has been broken, that anger has a basis in righteous indignation. It's not an anger that should linger for a long time and it's not an anger that keeps coming around in similar situations. It's an anger that can be settled with some form of a new agreement. The agreement is the issue in this case and a new agreement should solve the anger rather quickly.

If the anger you are experiencing doesn't resolve itself with a new agreement and it keeps creeping into your life, then the feeling that is left over is part of the second type of anger.

My experience with The Tool has shown me that this second type of anger is based on an internal fear. When I first began using The Tool I would have many issues that began with anger and as I explored them

Here is an important thing to remember about fear; our fears are never 'gone', and they don't just 'disappear' because we deny their existence.

The Tool

The Tool allows you to gently go within when you are angry or scared instead of lashing out at those around you.

deeper there would always be an internal fear as the basis of the anger.

If you are anything like me the hardest thing is to admit is that these angers are ours. They belong to us. We have learned to disown these angers with claims we are victimized, abused or somehow mistreated by someone or something else outside of ourselves.

It's so easy to deny that the anger we are feeling is *our* anger. If we deny it as ours, we can simply blame the anger on something or someone outside of us. You have heard it so many times in so many ways. "You make me so jealous I could scream." "You make me so mad."

The easy part of this 'externalizing' is we don't have to change. We don't have to look within ourselves for the answer. We can simply stand rigidly in our 'safe little world of the victim' and insist the world outside change.

The hard part is, if we won't look within, then we must get the outside world, or this other person, to be different. We mistakenly think that if we can only get the other person to change, then everything will be all right.

The only problem with this approach is when we try to force that person to be different, that other person needs to know exactly how they should be different in order for you to feel just the way you want to feel.

So we pound away at our mates and loved ones trying to get them to be a certain way because it is they who are making us feel the way we are feeling. They will never truly be able to understand how to behave because each time they think they have changed to please us, we are again feeling our internal fear , and accusing them of making us sad or angry, which again requires them to be something they can't know how to be and around we go.

Nothing really changes. The face can change but the feelings remains the same. You can get a new relationship but the feeling of betrayal remains the same. You can get a new job but now it's the new boss who's an asshole, just like the old boss.

Through all of this crazy look outside ourselves we can hear ourselves saying, "If only my lover would be dif-

You can get a new job but now it's the new boss who's an asshole, just like the old boss.

ferent or if only my boss could see what he is doing wrong then everything would be all right."

This external dance is completely dis-empowering. Your feelings become dependant on another's actions. You are angry at the behest of another. Will you also wait until some one or some thing behaves a certain way before your are happy? "If I could only find the perfect man then I would be happy." If I could find the woman of my dreams then I will become happy."

If you are happy dealing with life in this fashion then The Tool is not for you.

If you find yourself caught in this kind of trap and you want to change, The Tool can help. First, stop for a couple of minutes and consider that your anger is *yours! Own it!*

That is the first step. Then changing that internal anger will change the frustration and anger you are feeling. This internal confrontation is what The Tool is all about. The Tool allows you to gently go within when you are angry or scared instead of lashing out at those around you.

So if an anger keeps coming around to haunt you as a byproduct of similar events and circumstances, and you can't point to some agreement that's been broken, then the anger is probably based on an internal fear of some sort.

Don't take my word for it. See if it's true in your life. If you have an anger in your life that will not go away, use The Tool (or any other method you discover) to look for the truth of the anger. Be impeccable, and you might see that fear is probably the driving force behind it. And if it is not fear then what is it? Just anger? Look again.

These internal fears are not easy to see. They can be the same fears we have carried with us since childhood. They can be fed and nurtured until they become anger. The anger can then be fed until it becomes hate — all based in fear.

These are the fears that the Tool can help us understand and change.

Here is an important thing to remember about fear; our fears are never 'gone'

Different Varieties

Fear also comes in different varieties. You probably know the classics; fear of abandonment; rejection; control; being controlled; success; failure; the list is pretty long.

Some of these fears can be close to the surface and easy to see. Others are hidden a little deeper. The surface fears are the easiest to uncover, though they may screen another fear that is at the root of the stress or pain. In this way fears seem sort of 'layered' with so called surface fears hiding deeper fears underneath.

For example, we might be aware of a surface fear of being close to someone. "I am afraid of getting close to people."

This fear might be rather easy to see, however, upon closer examination we might find there is also a deeper fear of being involved 'layered' underneath the fear of being close. An even closer (more impeccable) look reveals another fear 'layered' beneath the two as a fear of being abandoned. This last fear can be the core, driving fear and is the one that the Tool can help discover.

These deeper fears are not always easy to look at and we can become very adept at hiding and denying them from ourselves. We can callous over them and delude ourselves into thinking they are 'gone'. It seems as though trying to get rid of fear is a desirable thing to do in our society. There is even a brand of clothing and accessories called 'No Fear'.

Here is an important thing to remember about fear; *our fears are never 'gone'*, and they don't just 'disappear' because we deny their existence. Our fears form the very foundation of who we are. They are among the first of our emotions and thoughts, and they are with us from childhood as our allies.

Fear is part of our animal instinct and has been created for our protection as human animals. Fear is a gift. When we sense danger, the adrenal glands pump adrenaline, and we are able to run faster and farther. We were able to run faster and farther in order to outrun the beasts and very real dangers of our early days as humans. Our fears are with us to help us survive, they are not there to hurt us.

We can try to dismiss our fears and hope they will go away or we can pretend we don't have any. But this

This book is here to suggest our fears are not an enemy to be battled but are indeed our friends and can be embraced as such.

The Tool

In general, in our society, the true physical threats are few and far between. There are very few actual lions, tigers or bears.

only succeeds in denying the existence of the very thing that is there to help us. This is another form of denial and it can be very painful if we choose to ignore our fears. Denying our fears can also be a most effective way of manifesting those very fears we fight so hard to ignore.

I bet that got your attention. Let's think about how that last assertion might be true. What if you had a fear that you would not look at no matter what the event. Why would that fear tend to manifest itself?

The easiest way for me to look at fear is simply as another part of who I am. I also see my 'job', if you will, as a human being is one of self-discovery. Within that self discovery I believe we have to look at all parts of who we are — all the parts! And part of those parts is fears. If there is a fear within and it has yet to be uncovered or recognized, it will strive to be recognized simply because it is a piece of the puzzle we call self.

These fears start out small and we can ignore them very easily. Then they grow a little larger. A little harder to deny but still not bad. The more we deny the existence of our internal fears and refuse to look, the larger they appear. This take many forms but mostly it will be in the form of some repeated stress or upset. Not the same event but the same feeling, over and over again.

If we get really good at denying our fear we can begin that sort of unreal, out of control spiral that we have all experienced. You know the internal messages. "Why can't I ever get it right?" "Why is it so hard to feel loved?" "No matter what I do it always comes out the same." Over and over we get the same emotional results no matter the person, the event, or the job.

So denying our internal fears can create event after event with the same reactive feeling imbedded within them until we are at the end of our rope and we scream, "STOP! ENOUGH!" The Tool allows for a way to say, "stop, enough," in a whisper instead of a scream.

Denying our fears can also be a most effective way of manifesting those very fears we fight so hard to ignore.

Emotional Fear and Physical Fear

We just listed a few emotional fears; fear of abandonment, rejection, control, being controlled, success, and failure. In this list one thing is constant, they are not *physically* dangerous. There is no physical danger to our bodies when we experience the fear of abandonment, rejection or the fear of success. True, fears can cause illness if ignored long enough but we won't be cut, bruised or killed by them. These are all 'emotional' fears, and physically harmless.

Since fear was given to us so we would be protected *physically*, from lions and tigers and bears, this creates a very interesting paradox. We can spend literally an entire lifetime defending ourselves against unseen and 'physically harmless' emotional fears.

Of course they are only harmless from an intellectual point of view. When we are feeling these emotional fears, they seem anything but harmless. The adrenaline pumps just the same for an emotional fear as it does for a fear that truly is physically dangerous. The problem is, we have distorted our emotional fears so completely, that the adrenaline rushes, and we are ready for fight or flight when we perceive we are threatened with something as 'harmless' as rejection.

We need adrenaline and there are, of course, true physical fears and dangers. These should not be ignored. In general, in our society, the true physical threats are few and far between. There are very few actual lions, tigers or bears. We do have speeding cars, slippery roads and falling trees. These are the 'real' threats in which we want adrenaline for extra strength and quickness. We don't need adrenaline when we imagine we will fail at a job or when we think someone will reject us.

When we begin to understand that our emotional fears are not dangerous, these fears will no longer have the power to control our reactions. When we are not controlled by our fears we get to play a little more with our lives. We might even find our lives becoming a little more joyous and creative in the bargain.

The Tool can give us a way to see the difference between physical fears and emotional fears. When we begin to see these differences we can also see we spend very little time in any *real* danger.

Most of the time when feeling fearful we are reacting to old, childhood, emotional patterns that have been distorted into life-threatening, adrenaline-pumping fears.

Remember that both fears, physical and emotional, are here to serve us as our protectors. The Tool can show us the difference and allow us to view both kinds

The Tool allows for a way to say, "stop, enough," in a whisper instead of scream.

of fear as our protective allies. It can let us see that the protection our emotional fears provided can be provided in new and more appropriate ways.

The Child Brain

So how do we get our emotional and physical fears so mixed up? It has to do with the make-up of our brains as very young children.

We often forget that as long as we occupy physical bodies, we are animals first and foremost and our survival instincts are supreme within us. Without those instincts, our bodies might not be around to observe any future creations.

One reason we can bury our true, joyous, creative selves so deeply has to do with this survival instinct and our nature as humans and human animals. One of these survival mechanisms takes effect the moment we are born.

This mechanism allows us, as infants, to have no ability to tell the difference between our own thoughts and those of the adults around us. This phenomenon lasts until 5-7 years of age. This ability is there for our protection as animals. Just as animals in the wild need to understand what to fear for their survival, the animal part of us is given this same ability.

As we were each growing up, our brains were set to receive our parents' thoughts and accept and incorporate them as our own. Think about that for a moment. All of our parents' fears and angers and all of their joys and laughters were accepted as our own thoughts!

This is great for our animal survival, because as young human animals, just like other animals in the wild, we cannot protect ourselves. At the same time we have to begin to learn what is dangerous and what is not.

As children, when we felt fear from the adults around us, we were obliged to accept that fear as our own. As the adults felt fear and the adrenals pumped adrenaline into their systems, the same things happened in our bodies and we were ready for fight or flight. We would be ready to run from a real, physical threat.

Again, this is all set up for our survival as animals and we can see how this would work well in a survival situation. Imagine a bear chasing the family and the

The Tool

This mechanism allows us, as infants, to have no ability to tell the difference between our own thoughts and those of the adults around us.

mother, knowing this is not a good thing, pumps adrenaline and is ready to run. The child, not yet knowing a thought of its own, senses the mother's fear and involuntarily pumps adrenaline to run faster and they are both able to outrun the bear.

The child may have no experience with bears and if the child hesitates even an instant to figure out if the situation is dangerous the child can easily become lunch.

The problem arises when we feel this same adrenaline rush and sense this same danger in situations that are not truly dangerous to our physical bodies. This begins to create the emotional fears we mentioned.

I remember that as a child, when I spilled milk at the dinner table, my parents yelled and screamed and seemed to be very angry. As a child I had no way of knowing whether that was a truly dangerous event. All I felt was the anger and fear, and with my child mind and brain I was obliged to consider it a matter of survival. The adrenal glands sent adrenaline through my system and I began to interpret spilled milk as a dangerous situation. The milk would spill, and I would feel the fear.

The part that doesn't work so well is the part that takes this 'survival' issue and applies it to our everyday lives. The fear that I would spill milk may cause one to become afraid to reach for things or make a mistake because the milk might spill or someone will yell.

Most likely my parents were only trying to teach me what was acceptable and what was not, or perhaps they were angry at some event in their day, or were frustrated about work. My child mind, however, could not see this and had no choice but to see this anger or fear as a fight or flight situation, for I couldn't tell the difference between my thoughts and those of the adults around me. In this way it was appropriate for me as a child to have the fear. As an adult, however, it just doesn't work. The fear was appropriate then, it is *not* appropriate now.

Of course, there are many other factors that form our lives, and as we grow up we are able to walk through a lot of these 'dangerous things.' Many experiences with spilled milk may cause it to lose its seeming danger rather quickly; however, there are other 'dangerous things' that may not lose their 'dangerous' nature quite as quickly. It's this distortion of the 'dangerous'

The Tool

No one ever taught us we weren't supposed to know the answers and that we were supposed to learn.

things that turns our emotional fears into perceived, adrenaline pumping, physical threats.

Again, there are some issues and events that really *are* dangerous. Our fear of these events is healthy and we would not want to change them. But we are bound to have a few distortions of what is, and what isn't, a truly dangerous event.

In our society we are taught that someone bigger and stronger and who feeds us, somehow, magically, has the answers to all of these strange mysteries. No one ever taught us we weren't supposed to know the answers and that we were supposed to learn. So as children, we might have developed a fear of not knowing the answers. We wouldn't attempt new things because we didn't already know the answers or the outcome. This is an appropriate fear to have as a child. But we might forget that as we went through life we *did* learn the answers.

We probably had a fear that we would fall down and crash when we were trying to learn to walk. This is another appropriate fear for a child, until the fear gets in the way of learning to walk. We probably had a fear of falling off a bicycle until we learned how to ride it. As soon as we learned how to ride, we had a different experience and the fear that was there to protect us was no longer needed. Instead of the fear protecting us we could protect ourselves by mastering bicycle riding.

If we have any fears that are getting in the way of participating with life, it might be a good idea to see if we can find another more active way to protect ourselves, instead of relying on the fear. If we can see that we are protected in other ways, we don't need the fear to motivate us. We can be motivated by desire, joy, pleasure and participation.

If we hang on to these fears because we don't recognize we have learned a new way, it can get painful. We might still think we need the right answers, or we may be afraid to try and ride the bicycles of our adult lives, or we are afraid to learn to run for fear of falling. Each of us as individuals has a few of these survival issues. You know, the place you can't help getting upset about— like when your children spill their milk.

These experiences, these 'buttons', the distorted fear-survival things, live within us as reactive, painful emotions. Without a Tool and the willingness to look at the experiences that create these sore spots, we are left living with our reactions to life rather than our interaction with life. Our fear that, at times, seems like such a burden, is there not as our nemesis and enemy, but as a protector and ally. It will stay with us and do its job as protector as long as we aren't willing to find another way to protect ourselves. The Tool will allow us to discover different ways to protect ourselves; ways that encourage active participation instead of paralyzing fear. It offers a way to see how fear and anger have served us and how they might be served in a different way. We might even be able to see that perhaps our fears are, in truth, our greatest allies.

Fear and Creativity

Another interesting aspect of fear is how it affects our creativity. By creativity I don't necessarily mean the creativity it takes to paint a picture or sculpt a statue but the creativity we use when we relate to each other as friends, family members, co-workers etc. It seems that as long as we are feeling fear, and there is adrenaline pumping through our systems, we are more reactive than we are creative. As long as we are being reactive it is very difficult to find new ways to deal with situations. When we react instead of participate we are presented with fewer choices and it is much more difficult to change the parts of our life that don't work.

Think back to a time when there was some sort of confrontation in your life. Do you remember the adrenaline rush? Do you remember there being a direct physical threat? If not then you were probably feeling an emotional fear. When in a confrontational situation and feeling the adrenaline, how creative do you remember being?

When the adrenaline pumped, were you able to interact with the other person and really participate with them? Were you able to create an interaction that discovered a win/win solution to your dilemma? Were you able to create a sense of equality or a sense of value for yourself and the other person? Were you able to create a different relationship than the one that existed before the confrontation? Or are you like me at times, and did you just clam up, afraid to say the wrong thing? Or did you react and spout off in a way that just made things worse?

Then a little time goes by and you are no longer feeling the fear and the adrenaline has subsided. An amazing thing happens. You think back on the event,

Without a Tool and the willingness to look at the experiences that create these sore spots, we are left living with our reactions to life rather than our interaction with life

The Tool

What's the most addicting drug on the planet?.......Yes, very good, our old friend adrenaline.

and for some reason all of these great possibilities and different ways to handle the situation appear. None would have been nearly as destructive to you or the other person as the reaction you chose. Somehow these new creative possibilities appear *after* the confrontation when the fear has subsided.

It is as if there a disconnect between creativity and fear. Like some part of us steps away while the adrenaline is pumping. See if it is true in your life. Sense when you get that emotional adrenaline rush and see how creative you truly are in that moment. The Tool makes it just a little easier to identify those fears, put them in their proper place, and get on with things with a little less reaction and a little more fun.

Conquering Fear

Or we can conquer fear. Think about that for a minute. How can you conquer a fear? Do you beat it into submission? Or battle it to the death? We have all done this one as well. We will drive our self through this overwhelming feeling of adrenaline to get to the perceived relief on the other side. But that is all there is —relief. Relief that there is no more adrenaline; relief that the danger is gone; relief that you have survived an unseen foe; and what's very strange, a wicked craving for more adrenaline.

All that has happened is the fear has been ignored and desensitized to the point of being stuffed so deeply within that it will never come out. No real personal discovery or revelation. Just an adrenaline high followed by an adrenaline low, needing an adrenaline high and so on and so on. Pop quiz. What's the most addicting drug on the planet? You can't buy it and you hardly know when you've taken a dose. Yes, very good, our old friend adrenaline. How many of your friends are addicted? Are you?

Embracing Fear

Our society teaches us our fears are to be feared, fought and overcome. We have been taught that our fears are adversaries. This book is here to suggest our fears are not our enemy to be battled into submission but are indeed our friends and can be embraced as such. This simply means to understand the reason the fear is there and embrace that reason.

The Tool can help us learn what our fears are, and see a way they can help, not hurt us. In this way our fears become our allies instead of our adversaries. Why would you want to conquer your ally? You wouldn't, of course. As allies our fears can begin to serve us and walk behind us to be called when needed, instead of bristling in front of us and our reacting to them.

The Magical You

These emotional fears that we have been discussing may be the very fears that are keeping you from experiencing the full you. You know the you I am talking about. The one that seems to lie just under the surface of the you that you project to others. The you that is happy and creative. The magical you that lives just under the surface of the pretend you that strives to protect itself from unseen danger, or the you that blows up at the kids for what appears to be no reason. The Tool can help you discover that reason, and give you ways to change.

Sometimes the magical you we are referring to is buried far beneath layers of fear and doubt that we have grown up with. This is very common in our society and it makes The Tool that much more powerful, although perhaps more difficult to begin to use.

The Tool may uncover things that are painful and that we think of as wrong. These are not easy things to look at. What's nice about The Tool is that it allows us to have a conversation with the part of us that does not view things as painful or wrong. It just looks at issues the way they are. It may be difficult to see things the way they truly exist, but it may also be time to start. The Tool offers a way to do that.

The Tool

How The Tool Works

This next section is designed to add a further understanding of how The Tool operates within our minds. It talks about the conscious and unconscious parts of our minds and their relationship with The Tool.

We human beings have been portrayed in psychological terms as possessing mysterious parts and pieces. We have names for them like the id and the ego, the superego, the subconscious, the unconscious and the conscious mind, among many other descriptive terms. To characterize who we truly are by using these old terms we have grown used to, probably does a disservice to the miracle that allows us to exist as human beings. Given that, I will nonetheless attempt a similar disservice by describing our behavior using the conscious and the unconscious mind as models. If it happens to have some relationship to what you know about the science of psychology then so much the

The Tool

better. If it doesn't, then take what you can from the descriptions given here and see if they apply to your life. Like The Tool, that is the only real test of their authenticity. We will begin by describing the purpose of the unconscious mind.

The Unconscious Mind

One of the jobs of the unconscious mind is to record all of our experiences. It does this without judgment and in a very logical fashion. The purpose of this "database" of information is to give us a foundation for our day-to-day lives. All of our fears, laughters, sorrows and every life experience is stored in the unconscious mind. As our experiences grow this database grows as well.

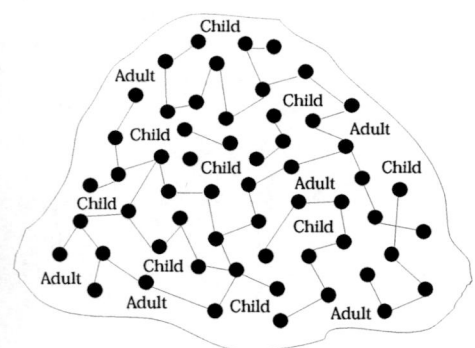

The unconscious can group a great number of experiences in the same place if they are related to a fearful event even if the events occurred at different times of our lives.

With each new event we experience, the unconscious mind checks within this database for similarities to any past event. If one experience has a similar look, or more importantly, feel, to another, then the unconscious will put that similar feeling experience into the same pile as other similar feeling experiences. If the experiences are driven by the feeling of fear, then the subconscious will put these fear-driven experiences in the same pile. A lot of us have a really big pile of fears.

There is, however, a slight problem that arises. The unconscious mind does one more thing with all this data and these piles. *It stores the data and builds these piles without a sense of time.* This simply means that it can't tell *when* an event happened. It is not interested.

You can see how this works by imagining a past event. Try it now. Close your eyes and think of a childhood event, either happy or sad. Now truly imagine the event. Try and recreate the sounds, the feelings, the smells. If you are willing to focus completely you will find the event is as real as if it happened 10 minutes ago. There is no definitive time-line in your memories, they are simply stored for your retrieval.

So the unconscious will not hesitate to put an experience that occurred as an adult into the same pile as an experience that occurred as a child. The only requirement is that there be enough similarities. In other words, our adult experiences can get grouped together with our childhood fears, if the unconscious detects enough similar elements.

Now imagine these great big piles of experiences grouped together because we haven't learned how to

The Tool

separate them. Now imagine a large pile of fear related experiences in your brain with each one attached to the others through a fear that had its roots in childhood, all dutifully built by an unconscious mind whose job it is to keep track of the events of your life.

The Conscious Mind

The difficulty with all this pile-building comes when the conscious mind enters the picture. The conscious mind is the mind that thinks, reasons, makes excuses, manipulates, and does all kinds of other things in order to do one thing—survive. Survival is the main purpose of the conscious mind. We use it (or it uses us) so we will be here long enough to see our next creation.

The conscious mind, in this quest to survive, 'checks in' with the unconscious mind's database of experiences to see if something is dangerous or not. The conscious will look at an experience and immediately access the unconscious to see how to react. If the experience is similar to a fearful place in the unconscious, the adrenal glands will pump, and you are ready for fight or flight. If the pile of similar, fearful

A new event that 'feels' like an old event can get grouped into your subconscious because the feelings are similar.

experiences is very large, the likelihood of touching a fearful looking spot is very high.

It might look like this: "Someone is yelling at me." The conscious mind accesses the unconscious to see if this is a time to pump adrenaline or not. The unconscious checks its database and finds a bunch of 'yelling at me' experiences. They are in this big pile that the unconscious has faithfully built. This pile contains *all* of the 'yelling at me' times, including those when we were children and the adrenaline pumped from our parents anger. These times all look pretty fearful and dangerous, so the unconscious reports back to the conscious and says, "According to my records, if someone is yelling at us, we should be frightened and pump adrenaline." The adrenaline rushes in a split second and you are ready to react.

This all happens quicker than it took to think about the next word in this sentence.

How The Tool Works

The Tool lets us communicate with our unconscious mind. With this communication we are able to break apart some of these large, fearful piles into smaller

The Tool

This "inner child" does exist, (here's a big but) BUT it exists more as an emotional experience than an event that can be clearly remembered.

piles without the same connection. It can do part of this by giving the unconscious mind a sense of time or better put, a sense of order.

This sense of order allows the unconscious to separate the childhood experiences and fears from the adult experiences. The two experiences are still similar, but *the Tool allows us to begin to see the differences.* There *is* a difference now between our adult perceptions and our perceptions as children.

Remember, we said the unconscious looks for *similarities* in order to build the proper pile or group. When we begin to see the *differences* in an impeccable way, this new, different look can allow the unconscious to put these experiences into different piles. The childhood fears and our adult experiences, which used to look the same to the unconscious, are now different enough that the two types of experiences don't have to be in the same pile any longer.

Now, instead of the conscious mind accessing *one* pile that previously contained *all* of the fear places, there are now two piles: one pile of childhood experiences and another of adult experiences—separate because they truly are.

After using The Tool, the conscious mind checks with the unconscious and there is a new pile of experiences; a new group that now separates the childhood experiences from the adult experiences. This process *does not* get rid of the experiences; it only holds them separate so they can be viewed differently. (You will see this separation as a function of one of the energies we will discuss shortly).

With this different view, you can have a different thought that was not available before, because of the fear connection. You might now say "Wait, I see more differences between this current event and what happened when I was a child. Now when 'someone is yelling at me' it doesn't *have* to be a scary place. Maybe the person is truly angry at something else and their fear has nothing to do with me. Maybe they truly are angry with me, but wait, I will check to see how I am connected here. Or maybe they are just having a bad day." With any of these new thoughts the connection is broken and you can build a new pile.

As these large piles get broken up and the conscious mind checks in to see how to react, it can now choose from a bunch of smaller piles instead of being dragged

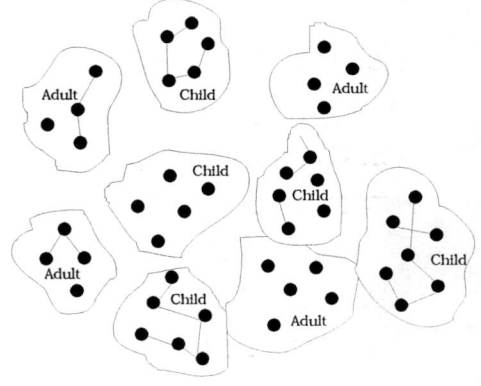

The Tool allows the subconscious to break apart some of these large, fearful piles into smaller piles without the same connection.

along reacting with the large pile of fear. If it is an adult experience, the conscious mind will check there and see that there is no real danger, and leave the childhood pile alone, for it is no longer appropriate.

So by using The Tool you can learn to approach life's experiences consistently. The conscious and unconscious mind begin to cooperate with each other and a piece of that consistent pattern gets placed in every pile. The more this consistent pattern is repeated, the more real it becomes. This is an active way to replace the inappropriate reactions with appropriate adult action.

Instead of being relegated to the way your unconscious had previously seen things you get the opportunity to say, "I *can* do it the way I have always done it but I don't have to, now I have another view and another way to do things. *Real* choices begin to appear.

Inner Child

Another key idea that allows The Tool to work is the simple yet powerful idea that all of the emotions we have ever felt or experienced are alive within us. This means that each emotional experience we had as a child is as alive now as it was then. You might have heard a lot of talk about the "inner child."

This "inner child" does exist, (here's a big but) BUT it exists more as an *emotional experience* than an event that can be clearly remembered.

These emotional experiences can be called upon at any time. Again close your eyes for a minute and think about the most memorable childhood experience you can recall. Now *really* feel it. It was so long ago yet somehow there it is. Is it real? When it occurred is not important. If you are feeling the emotion, it feels like it was yesterday or 5 minutes ago. These experiences are alive within us, (here's that big but again) BUT they are remembered as emotions, not as specific events.

We, as human beings, have the unique ability, and in a way, obligation, to put some sort of picture to what is more accurately remembered as an emotional event. We think we have the event nailed and we remember it so clearly but the picture we manufacture is most certainly a distortion of the true event.

We each probably have a few false ideas about reality based on some emotional event that lives within our "inner child."

The Tool

We then take the emotions we felt as children, view them through the filters of our life's experiences and we end up with a fairly inaccurate picture of what really occurred.

These events of our past that we imagine we see so clearly, and that we accuse of occurring just as we have them pictured, are interpreted by the filters we have developed as adults. These filters include a lifetime of experiences and thoughts and emotions that "color" the experiences in ways we can hardly imagine. We then take the emotions we felt as children, view them through the filters of our life experiences and end up with a fairly inaccurate picture of what *really* occurred.

Do you ever wonder why we are so concerned with what *really* happened anyway? Haven't you noticed that there are as many versions of an event as there are people involved in that event. Think of eye witness accounts and how crazy it is to think that two people could see the same event so differently.

Our version of what really happened is almost always different from another persons version. When we are children we have even less access to our logic and understanding of events so our perception of the events of our childhood can get pretty distorted.

For example, if you can remember a time from your past that was fairly painful emotionally, how accurate do you think your idea of the events are? If you are anything like me, you are probably convinced that your remembrances are perfect and there is no other way to look at the events. I remember thinking I was victimized by ruthless, uncaring adults who could not have wanted or cared for me. I distorted the fears I felt as a child and through my adult eyes, was still feeling the pain, only now I had years of experiences to back up my version of the past. In my case, I forgot that my parents had a version of what really happened as well.

The Tool has allowed me a gentle way to look at those past events and see that the emotional pain was mine. My parents weren't evil ogres, they were just doing the best job they knew how. My painful perceptions of being the victim—as a child—was probably pretty accurate. I might have truly been a victim as a child but there is no need for me to be a victim today.

The Tool offers a way to interpret those childhood emotional experiences in a more balanced fashion. It can't change what happened, but it can change your internal perception of what happened. When you look at the pain of a childhood experience The Tool can help you discern whose fear it was. If it was before the age of five, it was most likely your parents' or another adult's fear that is causing you pain. You just accepted the fear as your own. Does the event go away? No, but what if you had the thought that, "Wait, that wasn't even my fear and I have built this giant pile around this one false assumption of who I am." Does the event hold as much weight?

In my family, my mother would have liked my father to do more to provide for us and my father was stressed out and thought he could do no more. As a child I accepted both thoughts as my own. I thought, "I have to do more and yet I can't do more." This created a lot of anxiety in my life until I could see that the thoughts weren't even mine!

We each probably have a few false ideas about reality based on some emotional event that lives within our "inner child." If we are willing to accept that those emotions still live within us, it allows a way to discern which of those thoughts and feelings are valid today and which are not. The Tool can help separate the events into their proper places. Will it work right away? It depends on how you define work. It will not be all rosy and wonderful after a single session with

The Tool, but you will begin to see things in a different light and hopefully that different light will allow you to see yourself not as a victim of—but as a participant with—life.

The Tool

I might have truly been a victim as a child but there is no need for me to be a victim today.

Part 2

Chakras and The Energies

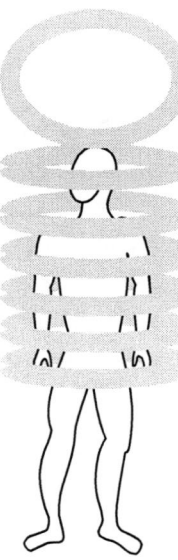

The Chakras

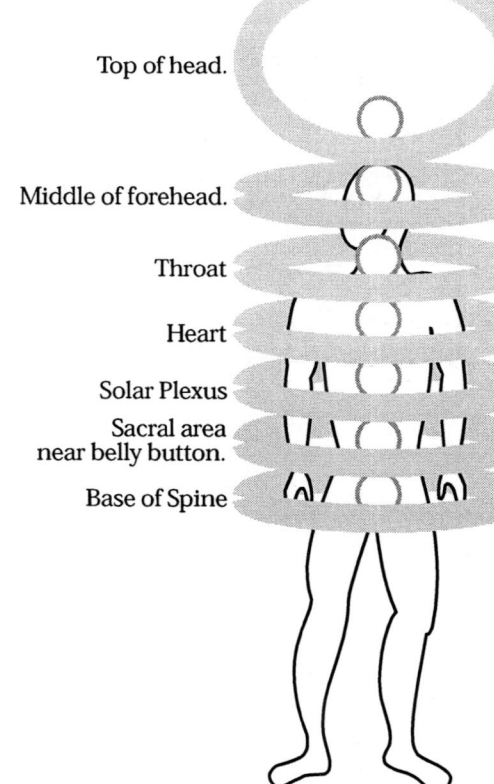

Top of head.

Middle of forehead.

Throat

Heart

Solar Plexus

Sacral area near belly button.

Base of Spine

Chakras

The following discussion of chakras is not meant to discredit any other teachings or ideas about chakras—only to present another option. If you have discovered an idea about chakras and energies that works for you, and it adds joy and balance to your life, then don't give that up too easily. Just perhaps look this idea over and give it a try.

Chakra is an ancient term used to describe areas in the physical body which focus and flow energy. Throughout the history of mankind they have been called vortexes, energy points, 'prana' centers and many other names. For the purpose of The Tool we will simply call them chakras.

There are many different ideas about the number of chakras there are, what color they are supposed to be, and their exact locations in the body. Also, the purpose of each Chakra has been interpreted in many different ways. Each of those interpretations have their value and some are rooted in ancient philosophies and spiritual teachings.

Again, this writing does not set out to argue the right or wrong way to see chakras or to present their function and location in an absolute form. If you find another way to see and interpret the energies within chakras, that interpretation will have value over and above all the ancient teachings you might ever discover.

Are Chakras for Real?

The existence of a chakra would be very hard to prove using scientific methods. They have never been seen by more than a select few who claim such abilities, though the energy of a chakra has been felt. This can be a really wonderful experience, but does it prove they exist? We usually need much more than a feeling to convince us that something is real, and to this date I know of no scientific proof that chakras exist.

So, for the purposes of this book, we would like to leave the discussion of the reality of chakras for those

It is too easy to get lost in the validity of an idea without giving the idea the benefit of its own validity.

who would decide such things. It is too easy to get lost in the validity of an idea without giving the idea the benefit of its own validity. Meaning, give these ideas and thoughts of chakras and energy a chance to live in your world. Apply them to your life. If they work they are real enough.

Matter and Energy

It has long been known that energy and physical matter have a special relationship. You've no doubt heard of Einstein's theory of relativity? It looks like $E=mc^2$. The 'E' in the formula stands for Energy, the 'm' stands for matter and the 'c' stands for the speed of light. What the formula means, in simple terms, is that physical matter is somehow composed of, and related to, energy. This alone is a very wild thought and deserves volumes beyond the scope of this book.

But if indeed physical matter is made of energy then the physical matter we call our bodies must have some relationship with energy as well. Chakras and The Tool are based on this relationship between energy and our physical bodies.

The Tool

The Tool proposes that energy comes in different varieties, each serving a different purpose in creation and the structure of physical matter.

This relationship of energy and physical matter usually revolves around energy as a singular commodity. Our modern scientists refer to 'energy' in the singular. The Tool proposes that energy comes in different varieties, each serving a different purpose in creation and indeed the structure of physical matter.

Those different varieties each resonate to a different part of the body and a different chakra within the body.

This concept of energy has many properties and we usually speak in terms of physical energy but the varieties mentioned above are concerned with both physical *and* emotional energy. We will explore both types of energy, but we'll discuss emotional energy first.

Emotional Energy

It might seem a little strange to talk about emotions in terms of energy, but think for a moment. Have you ever felt emotional energy? Someone walks into the room and you think, "Whoa, what was that?" 'That' was the 'emotional energy' of that person. You felt it.

You felt the energy as reflected by that person's energy fields or chakras.

These chakras carry emotional energy with them. We feel it all day long with every one we meet. It is the real method by which you pick your friends, your loved ones and your perceived enemies. We think we find our mates and lovers because they are pretty, or they have nice legs, but it's actually their personal energy field you are feeling. Their energy either works with yours or it doesn't.

How many gorgeous women or men have you met and just not 'clicked' with? It's an uneasy feeling you just can't shake. And how about the person you just can't stop talking with and who just feels so right to you. Those are the person's energy you are feeling.

Energy and chakras.

This energy ('E') that you feel is one part of the equation ($E=mc^2$) of us as humans. These energy fields or chakras form bands around us that might look like swirling donuts. Each of these chakras, and each energy associated with it, resonates to a different part of our emotional self. The sum of all the chakras working

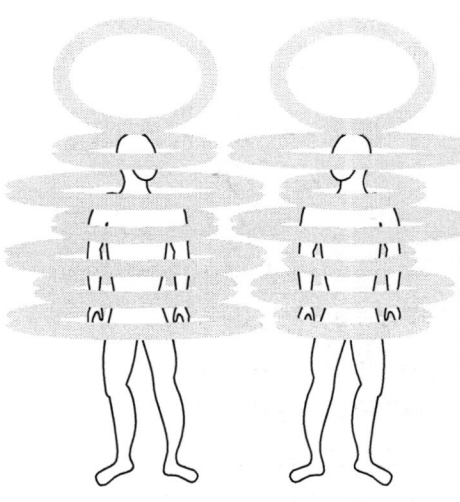

These two people might find themselves very comfortable with each other. Not because of their 'good looks' and great charms, but because their energies fit just right. Where one person is contracted in an energy another is expanded and those differences fit perfectly. Just the opposite can be true as well and you will sense a sort of repulsive feeling from those that do not match.

together creates a 'whole' picture of our emotional state. Sometimes this field of emotional energy is known as our 'emotional being.'

We carry different aspects of our emotions in these energy bands and, as just mentioned, we can sometimes feel when someone is happy or angry. These energy bands will also extend away from the body while another contracts itself inward toward the body. These extended or contracted energy bands are the ones we can feel most strongly.

As the energies extend inward and outward you can get a picture of how we 'feel' each other's presence through the chakras.

Physical Energy

The other aspect of energy is its physical nature. If we can imagine that Einstein was right, and that all matter is made up of energy, then we may begin to see that energy must also have some effect upon our physical bodies.

Our scientists are approaching this same conclusion though they speak in terms of quarks and charms and

What they are beginning to see, and what they will eventually discover, is that the energy we are describing does indeed exist.

other esoterica. What they are beginning to see, and what they will eventually discover, is that the energy we are describing does indeed exist. Not energy in a simple, singular form, but in varieties and flavors and that theses energy types form the very foundation of all that we know — including the physical matter we call a body.

Just as each chakra or energy type resonates to a part of our emotional body, each also resonates to a part of our physical body. The energies are focused in such a way that they effect one part of the body more than another. In this next section we name the seven basic energies we have been discussing and explore the different aspects of each one, including their relationship to the body.

The Tool

The Energies

Each of the chakras has an energy associated with it and each energy has a character or nature about it. We have divided our discussion of the energies into three areas. The first part has to do with the emotional nature of the energy. The second section deals with the extremes of those emotions and the third area relates to which cells within our bodies responds to each energy.

There are seven chakric points or energy centers. The energies that resonate to these points are vast and difficult to name at best but we have assigned each a name and function. Check out the chart to see the relationship between them.

The Energies

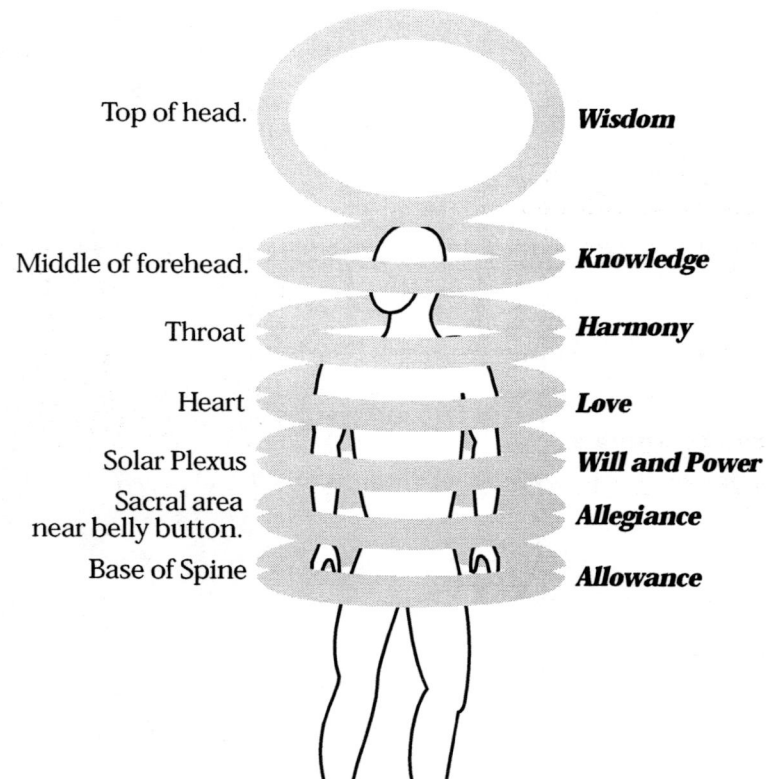

Top of head. — **Wisdom**
Middle of forehead. — **Knowledge**
Throat — **Harmony**
Heart — **Love**
Solar Plexus — **Will and Power**
Sacral area near belly button. — **Allegiance**
Base of Spine — **Allowance**

The Energies and their 'jobs'.

Allowance begins the flow and the focus for creation.

Allegiance gives the steps toward that focus.

Will and Power provides the self-control to take the steps.

Love discerns your true participation.

Harmony gives a broader view of the creation.

Knowledge contains all that has been in the past.

Wisdom shows all that may be in the future.

Allowance

The first chakra point is located at the base of the spine and the emotional energy that corresponds to that area is called Allowance. Allowance is the first energy to respond to our creativity. It says, "Yes, great idea! I will allow it," or, "No way, I will not allow it." It selects and focuses into the things you will and will not create. It provides the flow and the initial focus for any creation.

Emotions

In our emotional world Allowance is the place where we can allow too much or too little. Allowance is also the energy where we can begin to let go of judgment. Judgement of right and wrong and blame others or blame of yourself.

Extremes

If we are too allowing we can get scattered and unfocused. This is easy to imagine and we have all experienced this. If we are not allowing enough we can become judgmental, rigid and unforgiving. Maybe you have felt this disturbance in someone (or yourself) who has been very judgmental of others. Someone

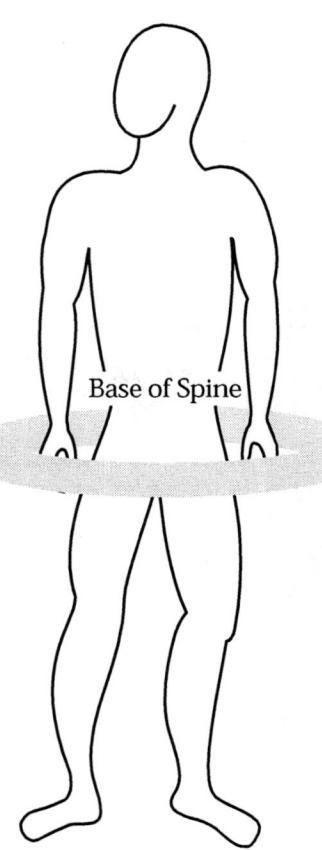

who will not 'allow' others to live as they choose. Or the other extreme may look like someone who allows too much in their life — not setting any limits.

The Body

In the physical body Allowance resonates to the organs that digest and utilize the food we eat. The kidneys, liver, intestines and stomach. What this means is that the cells that are located in these organs resonate to the energy of Allowance.

Allegiance

The second energy is known as Allegiance. It resonates to the sacral area of the body near the belly button. This is the second energy used in the creative process. Allegiance provides direction and begins to join things together. It builds upon Allowance with the steps that are needed to begin a creation. Allegiance will help to formulate a plan of action and together with Allowance helps create purpose. Allegiance can also show us what we will join with and what we won't join with.

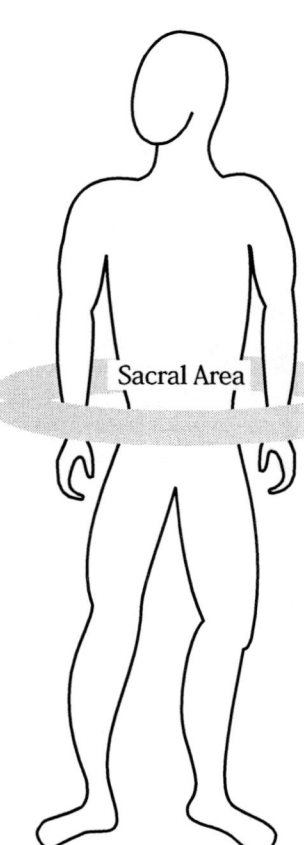

Emotions

When we get confused it can sometimes be from having Allegiance to someone else's plan or steps and no Allegiance to our own. How often have you done something because someone else thought it was a good idea? We might also have a fear of not joining with others. This joining is what Allegiance resonates to in the emotions.

Extremes

The extremes of Allegiance might be the feeling of joining with everything or joining with nothing.

The Tool

The Body

Allegiance resonates to the sexual organs of the body and to the endocrine system. You might be able to imagine the endocrine system also taking steps. Like a chemical factory that knows exactly how much of a chemical is needed at exactly the right time so we can function as human beings.

Will and Power

The next energy is Will and Power. It is centered in the solar plexus just below the center of the rib cage. Will and Power follows Allegiance and is the energy that moves thoughts and ideas together so that they become more physical in nature. It joins with Allegiance to help form intention. It is the binding energy that keeps things from flying apart. It is one of the energies that relates to gravity.

Any steps given by Allegiance must be 'willed' to happen. This is Will and Power's job. It is the action taken to accomplish a task.

Emotions

The emotional aspects of Will and Power look like different forms of control and cooperation. If we will not control ourselves, many times we feel as though we must control someone else. Also, if we will not control ourselves this can give the message that we need to be controlled.

Have you ever encountered someone who is just 'there', without a direction or purpose? Do you want to tell that person what to do just so they will not ap-

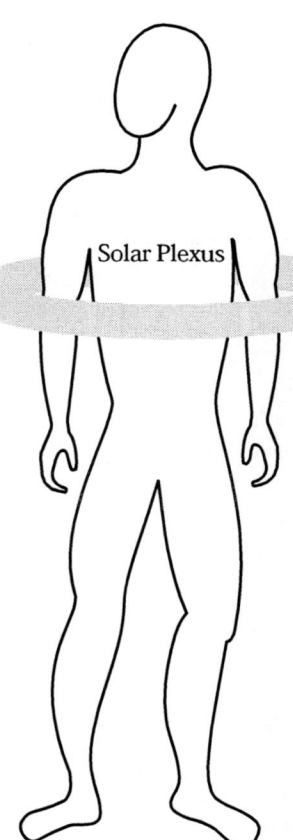

pear to be so chaotic? This is a natural reaction to persons not using their Will and Power to control themselves.

The other side of control is the desire to cooperate with ourselves and others who have the same interests and desires. One down side to Will and Power can be the feeling that you "have" to do something, and the up side is the feeling that you "get" to do something.

Extremes

The extremes of Will and Power might look, on the one hand, like an over powering, controlling person who refuses to control themself, or on the other hand like a floating, directionless person who likewise refuses to control themself..

The Body

Will and Power resonates to the bones, muscles and the connective tissues in the body. A lack of Will and Power can make the joints and bones weaker.

Love

The next energy is known as Love and it is located in the heart area. The energy of Love acts as a cushion that prevents Will and Power from completely forcing things together, so they will not become lost within themselves. Another way to think of Love is like a glue that holds things together so they can create, yet apart so that they may be perceived as separate. This is how we can be thought of as one people, for example, and still remain as individuals. No matter how close you feel to someone there will always be a thin film of Love that separates you; and no matter how distant you feel there will always be a connection through the energy of Love. Also if we didn't have the energy of Love, Will and Power would crush us into the earth and into each other.

After Will and Power has shown a way to control ourselves to get where we are going, we have to glue ourselves to the creation. Love is that energy glue that discerns and defines—how much glue or how little. Do you want to be close to a person or creation or far away? It's Love's job to discern the connection.

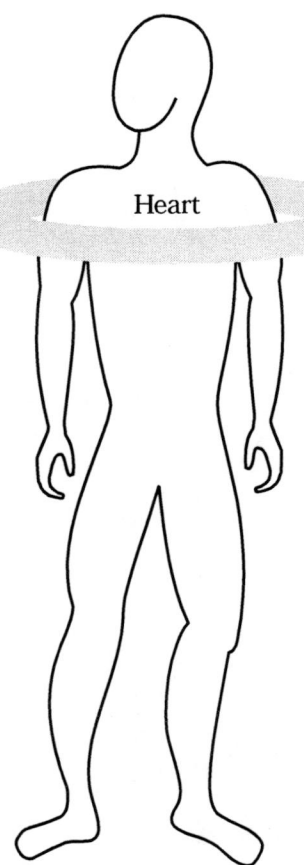
Heart

Emotions

To the emotions, Love can look like the ability or the inability to separate ourselves from others. It can help discern the emotions of others as yours or theirs.

Sometimes we find ourselves without enough of this separation when we think we are our jobs, for example. So how do we separate ourselves from our jobs and relationships, etc. and realize we are so much more? Perhaps a little more discernment with the energy of Love.

This is a very different view of what we know to be Love in our society, but as you begin to experience Love in this way it can become a wonderful new look at it.

Extremes

If there is too little of this emotional glue between ourselves and other people, this can be quite confusing. It might feel like all of the feelings of others are our own. We all have the feeling when we watch horrors on TV that we are connected to them in some way. We are connected but how much is the definition given by

Love. Too much glue or separation and we will be completely unaffected. Too little glue and we will think the horror is our own.

The Body

The energy of Love resonates to the heart, lungs and circulatory system in the body.

The Tool

Harmony

The next energy is Harmony. Harmony is located in the throat area. Harmony is able to balance all of the energies together into a combination that will create with the most efficiency. It is a sort of cosmic recipe book that knows the combinations of the energies that it takes to form the stuff life is made of.

Harmony tends to take a larger view that considers all of the energies, and its answer to an issue can be the closest to a 'final' answer that you will get.

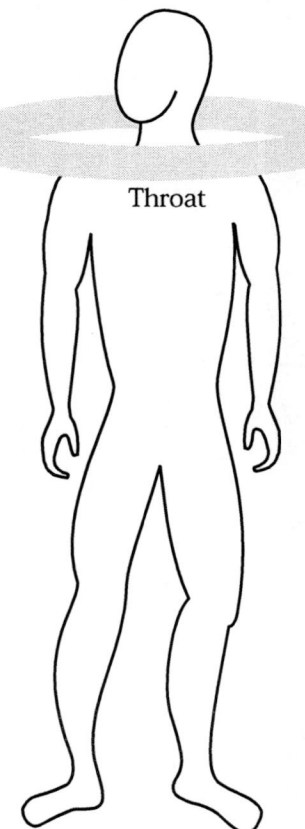

Emotions

Harmony is the energy that senses upset in our life and tends to act like our conscience. Harmony can also tell us how fast to move on a project or creation and exactly which steps to take and in which order. It acts as the coordinator in a way. Harmony can also tell us which of the other energies we might use more or less of to be in better balance.

Extremes

When there is very little Harmony in someone's life this can look like the need to have no upsets in life, ignoring that there is any problem. Too much Harmony might look like trying to create it in others and always trying to fix things for others.

The Body

In the physical body Harmony resonates to the immune system and it also has the ability to replicate cells in a proper genetic fashion so that, for example, a skin cell remembers to be a skin cell. When Harmony is out of balance in the body we may become ill more easily. When Harmony is spending a large amount of time trying to balance the emotional body it can get distracted from its job as a cell builder. In some cases it can be so busy with the emotions it will forget to tell a cell what its job is supposed to be. Having cells wandering around your body without a job can cause any number of illnesses.

Knowledge

The energy center for Knowledge is located in the middle of the forehead.

Emotions

To the emotions it is the energy of all that has been. Every part of who you have been is stored in the energy of Knowledge—and this means everything. This is the place where our soul keeps track of all the stuff that's been created. As you explore Knowledge you might even see things that happened before you were able to think of yourself as a person. Even these smallest experiences are stored in Knowledge.

Extremes

Too much of the energy of Knowledge can look like a know-it-all or the insistence that things must be the way they were in the past. Too little Knowledge might be a refusal to learn from, or consider, the past.

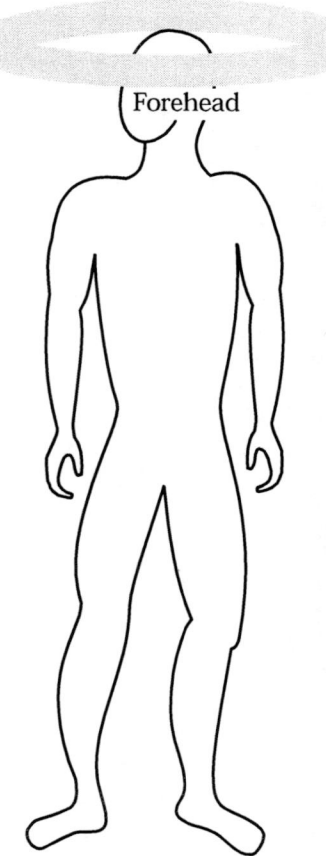

The Tool

The Body
Knowledge essentially resonates to the left side of the brain. It also resonates to general neurological and muscular functions.

Wisdom

The seventh energy is known as Wisdom. Wisdom aligns with a spot just on top of the head.

Emotions

This energy contains all the possible futures of you. Your imagination, your wonderings—the "what might bes" of your life.

Extremes

Too much Wisdom is dreaming without the doing and too little Wisdom is the doing without the dreaming.

The Body

Wisdom essentially resonates to the right side of the brain and is similar to Knowledge in regards to neurological and muscular functions.

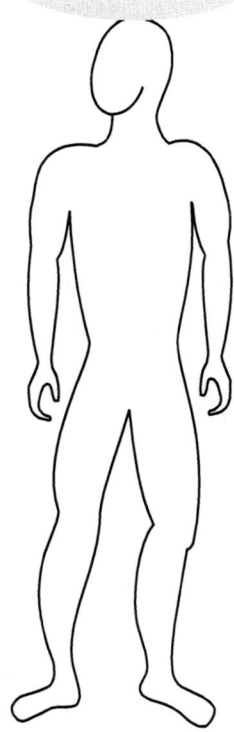

The Tool

Chaos

There is one more energy that plays a role in who we are. That energy is called Chaos. Chaos sounds pretty spooky at first and we have been taught to avoid Chaos in our lives. It does, however, serve a very valuable creative purpose. The energy of Chaos is unformed and unspecified and has a small piece of each of the seven other energies within it. It is like an empty space in which a creation may form.

In this way Chaos is a natural and necessary part of the creative process, and for this reason it may be considered desirable to have some Chaos in your life. This can be a great thing when that Chaos is working *for* you. When it is not working for you it can be very disturbing.

An example of when it is disturbing is when it is present in one of the other energies. Chaos is supposed to be unformed and unspecified, Allowance and the other seven energies are not. So if within Allowance there is no sense of what is and isn't allowed, or no sense of purpose and focus, it will be very upsetting to you. In this way Allowance is not the place for Chaos.

This is why one of the first steps with The Tool is to 'blow away' the Chaos from each of the energies. This is not to disregard and discredit Chaos, but to begin to form the seven other energies in balance and strength. This will leave Chaos to its rightful place as the emptiness that waits to be filled.

The Creative Process

As we discuss these energies you might be able to imagine how the creative process works. First, Chaos holds a space open for the creation. That can look like, "Hey I have an idea." At this point the idea is empty and unformed and Chaos holds a place for the creation.

Then through Allowance we find a focus. "Let's do this." The idea begins to take shape.

Then Allegiance, "I know, we can take these steps first."

Will and Power, "I will do the things Allegiance just suggested."

Love steps in and you decide, "I will do this part and this part. These are the parts that I see as mine."

Harmony gives you the sense of whether the idea is good for everyone or if it needs a little adjusting. Harmony might add, "You know I think we need a little more of this or that to make it work better for everyone."

Then this creation goes on to Knowledge where it is chalked up as an experience, (been there, done that) and then...

To Wisdom for the next possibility...Chaos creates a space...Allowance, Allegiance and on and on. If you think about it for a minute, it seems that Creation happens just like this anyway.

You might also be able to imagine what gets in the way of this natural creative process.

Let's take the same idea and Chaos creates the empty space..

This time Allowance says, "Lets do it but, Oh wait. I have a judgement that I cannot complete something once started. All stop on the creation train.

In Allegiance it might look like, "Yeah I don't really want to play, but if don't I am afraid I will be left out." All stop.

In Will and Power it can be a lack of self control. "I just won't find the time to do what I agreed to do." All stop.

In Love it can look like a confusion about where we stop as a person and where someone else begins. "I think that is mine to do but maybe it isn't." All stop.

Harmony can try to do too much and try to fix the disharmony of other people. "I can sense something is not quite right. I better fix it." All stop.

Knowledge might cause us not to take action if we think that tomorrow has to be like yesterday. "I have never succeeded before why try again." All stop.

Wisdom can look like dreaming, dreaming, dreaming, without the steps of action to start something. "I have another great idea, and another and another and another." All stop.

Each of these 'conditions,' if you will, have different words used for them in our society. The dreamer can be known as just that, "the dreamer," or 'spacey.' The person who gets stuck in Knowledge, thinking things have to remain the same, is the person you know who is very rigid in their beliefs or someone who won't try something new. The most judgmental person will not allow another their view of the world.

We have each probably experienced these conditions on some level. The hope of The Tool is that each of these personal challenges can be addressed and dealt with in a consistent, predictable manner that will add a certain stability to our lives and keep the personal creation train rolling.

The Tool

Part 3

Using The Tool

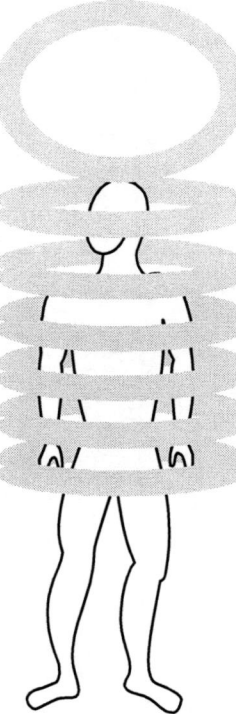

The Tool

Using The Tool

Now with all the talk about fear, anger, energy and chakras it is time to actually use The Tool. Not without a few more reminders and things to watch for, however. If you can't stand it any longer turn to page 112 and begin, but there is more information that can be very useful.

Rule number one—if you don't like the answers you are getting when using The Tool, GOOD! This sounds kind of weird at first and maybeeven a little intimidating, but the intention is to let you know that the answers you get may be uncomfortable and strange. Change is like that, and it's a good thing.

If you heard just what you wanted, or stopped using The Tool when you heard just what you wanted, what would the purpose be? It might just be an excuse to remain the way you are. There is nothing wrong with that, but if you want to stay the way you are, then The Tool is not for you.

This uncomfortable feeling also has a lot to do with the relationship between the conscious and the unconscious mind. The Tool communicates with the entirety of who you are. That includes both the conscious and unconscious mind. Since you are probably unaccustomed to hearing from all of these places in combination, you may get answers you don't like. Again, this is good. This means you get to change. The Tool offers a way to find out a little more about yourself than you knew before. Changing what you see is up to you. If you *do* want to change, you again may hear things you don't want to hear. Learn to celebrate those answers as well as the changes they bring.

Remember, it is off purpose to listen for answers you want to hear. You are looking for answers that are the truth of the whole you. Don't throw any answer away; don't try to make it reasonable so it 'fits'; don't try to massage it into a nice soft answer; don't try to take the sharp edges off of it; and don't try to figure it out in some logical fashion.

It will get figured out in your unconscious mind. There will be some piece of what you used to believe that will change. It's how you view that change that is important.

Not Always Words

As you use The Tool, not all the answers you receive will be in the form of words. Sometimes you will get a feeling or a vision, or who knows what. Whatever you get, remember it is *you* communicating with *you*, so don't throw your answers away. Your answers might be very short and appear to have no connection. Don't worry. You might even ask that as a question. "Why are my answers so short and seem to have no connection?"

Don't judge your answers to be better or worse than the answers you will see written in these pages. We have given some examples to illustrate the concepts. They are not examples of the 'correct answers.' Whatever the answer is that you receive, continue on and see what follows. Each answer is always useful in some way.

The Tool

I remember using The Tool and getting stuck right away in Allegiance. I couldn't get an answer and it seemed like I was struggling for the perfect answer. This struggle seemed to shut down the whole process.

I fought that feeling and thought it must be wrong. Then I learned a very important part of The Tool. Instead of fighting that feeling or ignoring it and throwing it away, I learned to use that 'wrong' feeling as the question. "Allegiance, what steps can I take so I don't feel like I have to have the perfect answer?" I found that this related to a large part of my life and my unwillingness to proceed unless I knew what the perfect direction was. The point is that every answer has a purpose, even if it's just a funny feeling. If all you get is a feeling, turn that feeling into the next question.

Might be Some Pain

Some past experiences may be painful to look at. When you feel the pain remember that pain can be short-lived. Here is a great jewel; *Within the vastness of the universe there is but a limited amount of pain and an unlimited amount of joy.* Isn't that a great thought? It's good to think of life that way when we come across those painful spots.

Don't Quit

Don't stop before you have visited with all seven energies. The Tool is designed as an interaction with the *whole* you — so talk with the whole you. There are pieces and parts that Allowance cannot reveal to you, and pieces and parts that Will and Power cannot etc. So go all the way through the process to get as complete an understanding as you can.

Colors Again

We mentioned colors earlier and there are as many different ideas about the "proper" color for a chakra or energy as there are people. We suggest that you avoid the absolute parts of the discussions on proper chakra colors. There also may be a very good reason that there is more than one interpretation of the proper color for these energies. Perhaps it's because we all see the colors a little differently. Each of us has filters and brain patterns that can distort the energies into a myriad of colors. So if you see a green color when you are visiting an energy, and another book or guru suggests you should be seeing orange, this is not a bummer and you are not doing it wrong. The color you see is your

The Tool

gift to you. You see green, so it is green for you. Do not throw it away.

You may not see colors at all. Don't worry, this is natural and you are not doing it wrong. It has to do with the makeup of the brain. Some brains are able to visualize differently than others. So explore and see what you see for the adventure of it. If you like, you may even fill in the chakra chart with your own colors.

The Perfect Question

It is really hard for anyone, other than you, to make a list of questions that is appropriate for you to ask yourself. Keep that in mind as you look over the suggested questions. The *intent* is the important thing.

The questions may differ in their exact verbiage each time you use The Tool. The questions seem to evolve along with the process. This can be both frustrating and magical at the same time.

Frustrating, because you just asked the 'perfect' question yesterday and today that same question falls on deaf ears and magical in that you get to discover the best question for today and today's situation. So there is no perfect question to ask, only the perfect discovery to make.

BREATHE!

The breath is an integral part of The Tool. It is suggested that you breathe *in* what you desire, and breathe *out* what is no longer appropriate. Breathe in your desires and breathe away your fears or the chaos from those fears.

Whenever you experience something that feels good, breathe it in, and whenever you feel something that is uncomfortable breathe it away. If it is very uncomfortable breathe it away in a forceful manner and do it more than once, if need be. Do not breathe in the 'positive' and breathe away the 'negative.' Positive and negative are terms that are unrecognizable to the unconscious mind. If you must use the terms define them so the unconscious knows what you are referring to. "I want to change this part of me, I consider it negative." "I want to keep this part, I consider it positive." Without that definition the unconscious will have no definable direction.

Positive and negative are terms that are unrecognizable to the unconscious mind

The Tool

You will also see a reference to breathing 'into' the energy or chakra. This can be done in a variety of ways. You can flex the muscles in the area of the energy (the solar plexus for Will and Power, for instance) on the in-breath and relax them on the out-breath, or you can reverse this process.

Here's a great one a friend of mine told me about. Imagine each energy as a band or doughnut that surrounds your body. As you breathe in to that energy, imagine the doughnut expanding. As you breathe out, imagine it staying the same size then expanding again with the next in-breath; like pumping up a tire. See how big you can get them. Or try just the opposite and see how small you can get them.

There are any number of ways to breathe 'into' the energies and it seems to only be important to focus on that area of the body when you breathe. It can sometimes help to touch each area as you focus on the energy as well.

It Feels So Good I'll Just Sleep On It

You may find yourself falling asleep when you use The Tool because it is sooooo.... relaxing. This is great for a good night's sleep, but not so good for changing your life. If you want to change the falling asleep part, use The Tool and ask whether sleeping might be a form of protection, and ask yourself how you might change it. Also, try crossing your legs or sitting in the lotus position, or any sitting position that allows the back to be straight.

Remember, this is your Tool to serve you, and the answers you receive are yours and only yours. Don't throw them away, and don't try to figure them out. Just go with the flow.

The Process

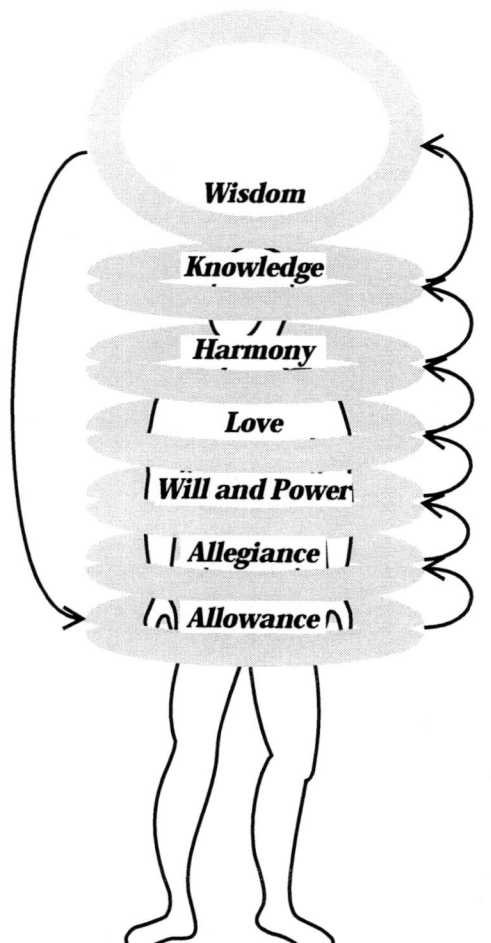

The Process

Begin using The Tool by first speaking with Allowance. Then up to Allegiance, Will and Power, Love, Harmony, Knowledge, then Wisdom.

When in Wisdom ask to see a smaller fear and take that answer back to Allowance and start the process over again. It is not recommended to stop part of the way through unless part of the answer is what you are looking for.

If you can stay focused, try to go through the process in this way 3 times, ending in Wisdom.

The Process

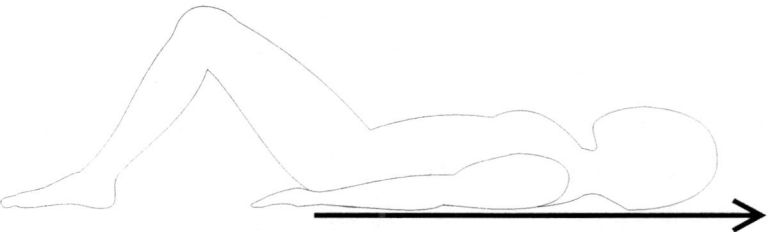

To begin, lie down on your back with your knees bent. This will insure the spine is straight and allows the energies to flow freely. You can put a pillow under your legs to keep them bent but not under your neck.

As you start to use The Tool you may find quite a few issues appearing through your day that you thought had been resolved. You may 'save them up' and look at each issue at night before you sleep. Don't worry, you won't forget what the issue was if your intent is to remember. This keeps you from having to excuse yourself to go use The Tool every time some situation angers you. If a situation does anger you, and similar situations keep on angering you, and you can't figure out why, that is one issue that can be put to The Tool. First, we will visit each energy in the body, then we will put an issue to The Tool.

Getting Acquainted

The best position to begin with is to lie flat on your back with your knees bent and no pillow under your head. This allows your back to be straight and the energy to flow between the chakras. You can also sit up in the lotus position or any other position that allows for the spine to be straight.

Remember the seven chakras or energies; Allowance, Allegiance, Will and Power, Love, Harmony, Knowledge, and Wisdom. This form of The Tool works in this same order. Beginning with Allowance and working up through Wisdom.

The first thing we will do is breathe into each energy center in the body in order to get a sense and a feel for that energy. After this first run through the energies, we will put the issue we have discovered to The Tool and see what we can discover.

Step 1. Allowance

Begin by taking a couple of deep breaths and blow out the air forcefully. We will start with Allowance. Breathe in and concentrate on the spot at the base of your spine (this was a hard place for me to find). Try flexing the muscles in this area as you breathe in. I ask for the energies as I do this and you may do the same, or just try breathing in and flexing the muscles. Now relax and breathe out, blowing out forcefully. Imagine the fears and judgments of the day leaving you with each out-breath. You may breathe as many times as you like. Begin to feel the energy of Allowance within your being.

Step 2. Allegiance

Now move to Allegiance. Try to sense where Allegiance is located in your body. It is near the belly button. Tense the area and breathe into this area and call the energy to you. I say, "Allegiance come into my being with the fullness of your energy," then blow away fear and judgments. Try placing your hand over your belly button and see if you can sense the energy of Allegiance.

Step 3. Will and Power

Do the same for Will and Power. Will and Power is centered in the Solar Plexus. Breathe in to this area and breathe away the fear and the Chaos. You may find words that work better for you to describe these things, but try to pick words that are similar. Remember the soul and the emotional energies do not understand good and bad, so don't breathe in the "positive" and breathe out the "negative."

Step 4. Love

Move up to Love and focus on the heart area, breathe in the energy of Love and breathe away fear and judgments. As you fill your lungs, imagine the energy of Love filling each and every cell of each and every blood vessel from your nose to your toes, to the tiniest vessels in your ears. Begin to sense the energy of Love.

Step 5. Harmony

Repeat this breathing pattern for Harmony at the throat chakra. Breathe in Harmony to your being and breathe away all that is disharmonious. See if you can feel the energy as it courses through your body.

Step 6. Knowledge

Now breathe to Knowledge in the middle of the forehead. Ask that you remember all that is known of you and breathe away the Chaos.

Step 7. Wisdom

Now breathe to Wisdom located in a spot just above your head. Breathe in all the possibilities and breathe away the fear and pain.

You should be quite relaxed at this time, but remember this is an active contemplation. This wonderful relaxed feeling is, in and of itself, very beneficial to the body. However, it is the emotional body that you are visiting, and The Tool has a purpose. You may rest here and just savor the feeling, but if you have some aspect of your life you would like to change, go on to the next part.

The Issue

Now we will place an issue to The Tool. Let's say you have discovered a situation that angers you, and you realize it is not because someone has broken an agreement. This probably means it is based on an internal

The Tool

fear. You also have decided to change this situation. Remember this does not mean changing the other person, but changing your perception of the anger and fear.

As an example, let's say that every time someone gets close to you in a relationship you find a way to destroy the relationship and drive that person away. It is very painful and you want to change the painful parts.

Let's Start

Now let's put the anger about destroying relationships to The Tool.

1. Allowance

We will begin breathing into Allowance and ask to see the truth of this situation. You might say, "Allowance, why do I have so much anger over losing my relationships." Allow yourself to see the truth without judgment. Take away the right and wrong of it and this will release it and allow it to be changed. You may get words or a picture or just a feeling. (If you won't allow yourself to listen to the truth, you might ask why and

Take away the right and wrong and this will release it and allow it to be changed.

allow yourself to see that.) Now blow away the judgments for they live in Allowance.

What do you see? What do you feel? What appears to be the truth?

When you have discovered the truth you can thank Allowance. In our example, we may discover the truth has to do with an anger and fear of being close to people. It seems to serve as a form of protection from getting hurt.

You might now ask, "How else can that fear be served; how else can I find the same protection?" Allowance may suggest that you cannot truly be hurt, there is no physical danger. It may even be that the pain comes from *not* being close to someone. Allowance may suggest that you get closer to someone—for it's from being close that you can feel the joy and pleasure of a relationship.

In this example the fear has served and protected you by keeping you separate from people, and Allowance has shown you that you may gain the same protection by actually getting closer to people. Now you have a new focus or desire. You have seen that the fear protects you from the possibility of pain, and Allowance has suggested another way you can protect yourself from pain, a way that is an active participatory way, not a paralyzing, reactive way. Allowance has suggested to get closer to someone.

With Allowance, ask to see the truth of your fear, and see how you may serve that fear in another way. This gives you a new direction or desire.

2. Allegiance

You could stop here but now you need a plan. You need some steps. Of course, that happens to be the job of Allegiance. So you take your desire and ask Allegiance what steps you may take to achieve your desire.

Breathe into Allegiance and ask for the steps to fulfill your desire to get close to someone. Following this same example Allegiance may tell you that you could say what your feelings are more often and you could just stop for a second and listen more carefully to someone. Focus on your relationship with someone.

Allegiance gives you the steps.

The Tool

3. Will and Power

Now that you have a plan you need the Will and Power to carry out your plan. This is Will and Power's job. Breathe into Will and Power and ask, "Show me how I can cooperate with myself and take the time to listen to others." Breathe out the need to control others. Will and Power may suggest you add a little discipline. Stop talking and wait your turn to speak.

Will and Power gives us the Will to take the steps.

5. Love

The next step is to breathe into Love. Love is the glue that binds us all as one, yet holds us separate so that we may discern our individuality. Ask Love to show you how stopping to listen will bring you closer. Love may say that your closeness to another is not something to be feared but a thing to cherish. The choice of how close one is to you is always yours. Also know you will always be connected in some way. Simply recognize this as the truth.

Love allows us to stand aside without removing ourselves.

6. Harmony

Next comes Harmony. Harmony is the energy that looks at the big picture and can, many times, give you insights into your relationship from another's perspective. Breathe into Harmony and ask that you see the large picture, that you may see more of the truth.

Harmony may say, in our example, that the fear you feel is not yours alone—that your friends also may feel this same fear. The purpose is not to accuse the other or to use this Knowledge as a weapon, but to see that this is also part of the truth of your relationships.

Harmony can give a view of the bigger picture.

6. Knowledge

Now breathe into Knowledge. Knowledge is the energy of all that has been. All the events of your life are recorded in Knowledge. Ask Knowledge to show you all the times in your life that you have felt the same feeling or seen the same things. Knowledge will show you all the times you were afraid to get close and the pain of that separation. A look into Knowledge can be an amazing thing and a very emotional experience. Don't doubt the images that can come up, even the ones that look like you were too young to remember. Knowledge remembers.

You may find yourself crying or laughing quite uncontrollably. Allow these feelings to flow through you and thank them for their gift. These are your experiences, so breathe these events into your being and cherish them, for they are who you have been. Now breathe them away from you and know that they are your yesterday not your tomorrow. Tomorrow can be different.

Knowledge lets you see all of your past.

7. Wisdom

Now breathe into Wisdom—the what might bes. All the possibilities for your life live within Wisdom. At this stage it is most likely you have not discovered the whole truth of your fear. Ask Wisdom to see the effects of your new actions.

If you get an answer or feeling that has some anxiety or fear, here is the place to ask Wisdom to show you this smaller fear, for these fears live in the what might bes also.

Wisdom shows you the possible 'what might bes'

The Tool

In our example let's say Wisdom discovered another, smaller fear. Wisdom has uncovered a fear of being 'found out' if you get too close to someone.

The answer may not make the most sense. Don't analyze it!! Put the answer to Allowance.

Allowance, "What is the truth of my fear of being 'found out?'"

Allowance might say, "You are afraid of revealing yourself to another for you might be attacked. There is no need to reveal yourself to another, only to yourself." Again you have a new direction. You need a plan.

Allegiance, "What steps do I take to reveal myself to myself?"

"You are taking them. The contemplation will reveal you to you."

Will and Power, "How can I cooperate with myself and do this contemplation?"

"Simply set aside some time during the day to do it."

Love, "How will I know which parts are mine as I do this contemplation?"

"It will come as a sense. Follow your sense."

Harmony, "What is a bigger picture I can look at?"

"Think of others as you do this contemplation and your effect on others."

Knowledge, "Show me all the times when I did not think of my effect on others."

"You might see many times you neglected others or ignored their needs or many other things."

Wisdom, "Is there a smaller fear?"

"You have a fear that you have no effect."

Allowance, "What is the truth of this fear?"

"Your fear that you have no effect alienates those around you as you accuse them of having no effect as well. This causes you to not listen too closely."

Allegiance, "How can I see the effect of others and listen more closely?"

"Simply notice your feeling around others. That is effect enough."

The Tool

Will and Power, "How can I control myself to notice my feelings around others."

"Slow down and stop to notice."

Love, "Show me how I might discern my feelings from others around me."

"Feeling, sensing, practice."

Harmony, "Show me the bigger picture.

"Remember as you are effected so you are effective, as are others around you."

Knowledge, "Show me all the times in the past I have been ineffective or judged others to be ineffective."

The Tool might reveal a small child screaming in the wilderness, unheard and disregarded. Parents going about their business as if the child were not there. You might also see a time where you were too effective, trying to compensate for your thought of being ineffective. All of these times were in the past. Blow them away for they no longer need be true.

Back to Wisdom for a smaller fear. Then to Allowance etc. Always end in Wisdom.

The Tool

The previous example is a real example of The Tool and how it can work. It was done while the book was being written in a spontaneous a fashion to illustrate the nature of The Tool.

Your questions and your answers will not be the same. Secondly I am very practiced at The Tool and the answers come fairly clearly to me. Your answers may not be as clear as they appear here or they may even be clearer.

The important thing is to see the progression of the process. Each question gives an answer which forms the foundation of the next question which gives an answer that forms the foundation for the next question and so on and so on.

What did the process reveal? Notice that the issue began as the fear of being close and ended up being about effect. It is hard to get close if you disregard another's effect on you, and vice versa. There was no way to figure that out logically and a couple of times the answers threw me and was in the very familiar position of needing to know the right answer but I continued on. That is the trick. Keep going even though it stops making sense.

The Tool

This is also not the time to get too deeply into analyzing what you have learned. Trust that you will see things a little differently and watch for the change. The change you are seeking may be subtle, but it will be there.

Remember, the first time through The Tool forms a sort of foundation to go through the energies again. So whatever answer you get from Wisdom, take it back to Allowance to see the purpose, Allegiance to find steps that are different, to Will and Power to see some actions, to Love to see that it is a new creation, to Harmony to see that it does not harm anyone by taking the actions, to Knowledge to record it as a new way to be and to Wisdom to see another possibility.

When you are finished with this session of The Tool you should find yourself in Wisdom and you may feel pretty far 'out.' This last time in Wisdom you can ask this energy to allow you to begin to feel your body once again. Feel your toes, your legs and every part of your body. Then slowly open your eyes or fall fast asleep, whichever is appropriate.

Third Time Is A Charm

The greatest benefit will come after the third time through all of the energies. Going through three times can take the distractions or fears and begin to narrow them down into a more focused point. The first time through gives you a big picture, the second time narrows that a little by showing a smaller fear and the third time gets to the nitty gritty. This nitty gritty is the place that is the most creative and allows you to take an action that is different than one you had taken before.

We hope the example gives you an idea of how this tool can work. We can take the fears that immobilize us and bring us pain, and find ways to protect ourselves in the same way by acting instead of reacting.

Imagine what it would be like if you could spend your day without the distractions or angers of your job or relationships or whatever. This Tool can help turn those distractions into allies and add creativity to your day.

To review

STEP 1. Ask Allowance for the truth without judgment and to reveal a desire within the fear. A new direction.

STEP 2. Ask Allegiance for the steps toward that desire.

STEP 3. Ask Will and Power for ways to control yourself and cooperate with your desire.

STEP 4. Ask Love to define your involvement. How close are you to this creation?

STEP 5. Harmony can give a bigger picture.

STEP 6. Knowledge will show you all of the past.

STEP 7. And Wisdom will show parts of the future.

You Can't Do It Wrong

Don't worry if using The Tool is difficult at first, and don't think you are doing it wrong if the answers you get aren't as clear as the ones written here. These answers are for illustration purposes only as it is hard to relate the concepts without giving complete answers. Some people don't even get words, just images and feelings. That's OK too. Remember, you can't do it wrong! You can only not do it.

The method just described is a great way to begin, and if you find that The Tool suggests another way to you, try that new way by all means. As you begin to trust yourself and your relationship with The Tool you will find there are very few limits to what can be discovered.

Don't expect dramatic changes. This can happen, but most will be subtle changes, such as you didn't yell as loudly or as quickly as you used to, or you did the thing you always wanted to and it wasn't scary. Look for the subtle changes. They will appear if you are willing to look. In our example you may suddenly realize that you actually listened to the person talking to you and found yourself feeling closer.

What If You Don't Get Answers

I've used The Tool and have gotten answers that are clear and concise and have followed the formula just right and I can write down the answers and pat myself on the back with, "Oh boy I'm doing a great job and I have this Tool thing figured out."

The Tool

Other times I am so anxious that I can barely put a question to Allowance, and not even remember the answer if there was one, go on to Allegiance and ask 'who knows what' and go on to the next energy, doing no more than merely visiting each energy. I'll have the thought that I have done it all wrong, of course, but somehow the next day things are different. A little clearer, a little less anxious. So if it looks like you are getting no useful answers, hang in there no matter how it appears to be going.

If you think you are not getting answers, there are a couple of things to remember. The first is that you *have* gotten an answer, it can't be avoided. It might just be that it raced by so fast that you couldn't grab it and expand on it. If you want an answer and the process works better for you to have a *real* answer to use then make one up. Make one up? Yes. This made-up answer probably came from The Tool anyway.

Another thing to remember is the focus and purpose that is set by Allowance. If you don't get an answer, use this focus for all of the energies. As an example if you asked in Allowance, "Why do I get so scared when my mother yells at me?" and did not get an answer (or at least no answer that you can recall) simply go on to Allegiance and ask a question related to the focus given by Allowance. "What are some steps I could take to see my mother's anger as a help?" or "What steps can I take to see my fear as a benefit to me?" Just design the question around what Allowance has started with. In W & P do the same thing if you did not get a clear answer. "How can I control myself and cooperate in a way that sees my fear as a help?"

Our logical mind thinks that this will not work, but there is some kind of magic that happens even if it looks all wrong. I try to remember this last part when I am the most anxious. Stay with what you have presented to Allowance and go through *all* of the energies. Don't try to figure it out.

It's Not Easy

The Tool is not necessarily an easy thing to do. If you are having trouble, just be patient and enjoy the parts that are working for you. From childhood we have been taught entirely different ways to handle situations, so this technique may take some practice and some getting used to before you feel completely comfortable with it. After all of the years of living our lives

The Tool

without examining the reasons for our reactions, this can be quite a change. But if change is what you desire, the key to that change lies within. This tool will help you unlock the truth of you, and as you use it you will begin to see the strength, the beauty and the wonder that you truly are.

More Tools

There are a couple more forms of The Tool that can also be really effective. These are mainly focused on the physical body, though you can ask questions at any time you like.

The Tool For the Physical Body

Each of the energies resonates to different cells within the physical body.

Allowance resonates to the area at the base of the spine and also the organs that filter and cleanse the body.

Allegiance resonates to the sacral area, the sexual organs and the endocrine system.

Will and Power resonates to the solar plexus, the bones, muscles and connective tissues.

The Tool

Love resonates to the heart, lungs and the circulatory system.

Harmony resonates to the throat area and the immune system.

Knowledge resonates to a place in the middle of the forehead and to the general muscular and neurological system.

And **Wisdom** resonates to an area slightly above and outside of the body and to the same general muscular and neurological functions.

It may take some time to feel the energies within your body or you may find them quite easily. There is always some change with this technique, but you have to practice before you can feel all the subtle little feelings. If you think you have done it wrong because you do not see fireworks after each breath, just lay there after you go all the way through the energies and see if you can ever remember being that relaxed. Again, you can't do it wrong!

This form of The Tool begins in the same way as the previous form. Breathe into each of the chakras and breathe out the judgment, fear and chaos.

Allowance

Beginning at the bottom, or the root chakra, ask Allowance to fill your physical being with the fullness of its energy. "Allowance, cause all the cells within my body that resonate to your energy to be filled with your energy." Breathe in Allowance. Now lie still and sense your body. What do you feel? Allow the energy to come to you. It may be very subtle or it may be quite profound. Breathe with it. Sense the energy as it resonates to your body.

Allegiance

Do the same with Allegiance. Sense the energy. Breathe more than once or even try a few rapid breaths and feel the sensation. Try it while flexing the muscles in the belly button area while breathing in, then try it while relaxing these muscles while breathing in. What do you feel?

Will and Power

Breathe into Will and Power and flex all the muscles in your body and see what you feel. Ask for Will and Power's energy to energize all the cells within your body that resonate to Will and Power.

Love

As you breathe into Love feel your lungs fill with the energy of Love. Ask that all the cells that resonate to its energy become energized. Imagine the energy filling your lungs, moving into your veins and arteries, expanding, moving out to your arms and legs and into the smallest of capillaries within your body. Can you feel the energy in your fingertips and in your toes? Can you feel the beat of your heart? This is the energy of Love.

Harmony

Now breathe into Harmony and sense your immune system. Imagine your lymph glands (some of these are located in your neck, under your arms and in your groin area) becoming energized and pumping white blood cells and all of their protective energies throughout your body. Sense your throat and the energy flowing throughout your body. Be still and sense the body. Is it a little more alive, a little more excited?

Knowledge

Now breathe into Knowledge. Breathe to a spot in the middle of your forehead and ask the energy of Knowledge to energize your body. What do you sense?

Wisdom

Lastly, breathe into Wisdom, and ask that Wisdom energize the cells in the body and sense the energy. Do you feel larger? Expanded? More aware?

This is a gift to your body and the body can guide itself. So listen to your body. If it wants to stay in one of the energies for a while longer then keep breathing there to see what comes up. This is great for tuning the body after a hard day's work and if done with regularity, the body might need much less sleep than usual.

The Long Breath

A good way to finish each of these contemplations and to come back to your body is a breath called the Long Breath. It is also a good balancing breath for the body.

The first step in the Long Breath is to quiet your mind and begin to feel all the parts of your body. Focus on

The Tool

your heartbeat and begin to breathe in its rhythm. If you can't feel your heartbeat try breathing out forcefully a number of times and see if this helps. Do not feel for the heartbeat in your wrist or other pulse point, feel for the rhythm of your body as a whole.

Begin to count the beats, and with the 'in' breath count seven heartbeats. Now with the 'out' breath count seven heartbeats. Seven beats in and seven beats out. Continue with this rhythm until you feel an evenness in your breath and your body.

Now begin to focus on your toes. Feel every part of them, every cell, every muscle and every bone. Move up to the ankles and do the same thing with every part of your body, embracing every cell. Continue with the breath; seven in and seven out. After you have visited every part of your body (don't forget the earlobes) slowly open your eyes and see if your world isn't a little different. Do you feel relaxed? This breath is great for sleeping too!

The Energy Dance

This next form of The Tool is an active form. It is meant to be used while moving or dancing to the energies. This 'Energy Dance' is a great way to start the day, and the emotional form of The Tool first discussed is a good way to end the day.

Within this dance you don't necessarily ask questions though you could. It is mainly a way to move your body with your energies. You begin this dance in the same way we have previously described, starting with Allowance, and working up to Wisdom. As a form of dance it's a really difficult thing to describe in a book like this. I hope the drawings help, though if they are too vague just have at it and see what flows.

Imagine this energy dance to be similar to Tai Chi. The difference is you do not follow someone else's idea of the proper body movements, you follow your own.

The Tool

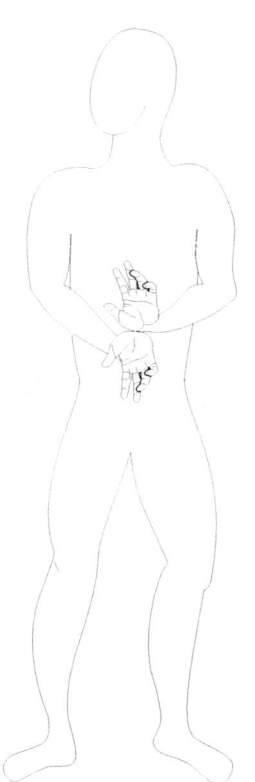

Figure 1 Begin the Energy Dance by breathing into each energy with the palms facing out and the wrists together. Place your hands at each energy and see if you can feel each energy.

Like all forms of The Tool, this is as unique as you are and that makes it even harder to describe, but here goes.

To Start

A good place to start is with your feet about shoulder width apart. Just get comfortable and secure. Now focusing on Allowance at the base of the spine, draw your hands together as you breathe in and hold them together at the wrists, palms outward and feel the energy. (See figure 1.) It may take a while before you can 'feel' the energy but just stand there for a moment and sense your self. Now breathe out and move your hands away from your body in the area you would imagine Allowance to be. (See figure 2.) Imagine the energies surrounding your body like large donuts. What do you feel? Can you sense the energy? Try using the technique we described earlier with The Tool and see what you feel.

Now do the same thing in Allegiance. Breathe in and draw your hands together and breathe out and push your hands away from your body. This time as you breathe out move your hands away to one side and take a step that same way. Do you notice anything?

The Tool

Wow, it feels so easy to move to the right but really weird to move to the left? (Or vice versa?) Congratulations, you are beginning to sense the energies and this morning they want to move you to the right. That simple? That simple.

Now move up to Will and Power. Your muscles and connective tissues resonate to Will and Power. Tense all your muscles as you breathe in. What do you sense? What do you feel like doing? Jumping? Jump! Spinning in a circle? Spin in a circle! Nothing? Do nothing! Breathe out and move as you feel.

Now breathe into Love. Perhaps cross your arms in front of your heart. Perhaps stretch them as far as they will go. How does your body feel like moving? Breathe away the fear and judgments for the day. Dance!

Now to Harmony. Try some movements that resemble figure eights—vertical eights, horizontal eights and sideways eights. Breathe in and sense Harmony within you. Does Harmony want to dance? Spin in a circle. Which way spins with the energies? Which way spins against them?

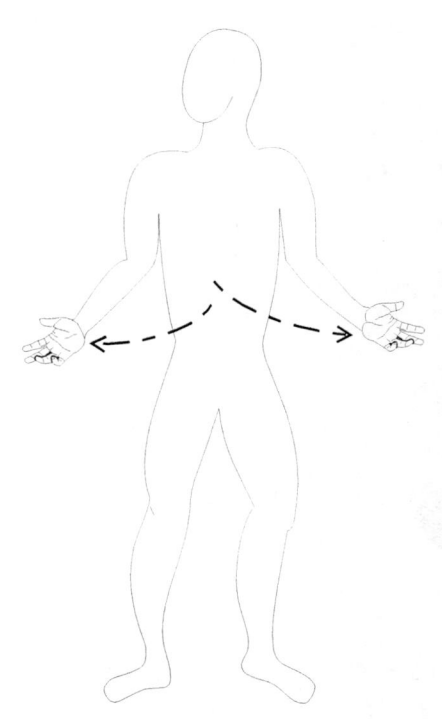

Figure 2. Breathe out and move the hands away from the body in the region of the energy. Sense the energy.

The Tool

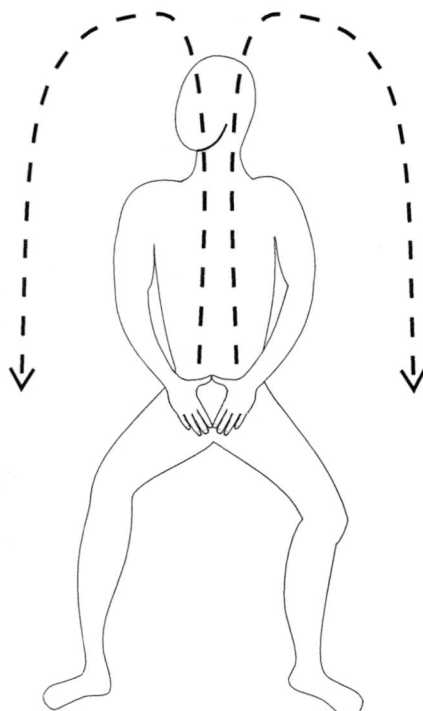

Figure 3. When you get up to Wisdom, form your hands, palms inward, with the thumb and forefingers together making a little triangle in the middle. Breathe in slowly and move the hands up through each energy. When you reach the top let your hands and arms fall to the sides and for our your breathe. Repeat a couple of times. Great energizer!

Knowledge will move you in a new way. Just sense the energies and move with them.

At Wisdom begin with your feet at shoulder width, (that is if you can stop dancing) hands open with your fingers together. Now place them in front of Allowance, palms facing you with the thumb and forefinger of each hand together. Form a little triangle with your thumbs and forefingers. (See figure 3.) Got it? Now tense all the muscles in your body and slowly breathe in moving your hands and their little triangle up in front of your body.

Feel them pass each chakra. Palms still facing you. When you reach the top, turn your palms outward. Now let go of your hands and quickly drop them in a wide circle away from your body and breathe out all the way. How does that feel? Do it again. What? You get to Wisdom and feel like doing something different? Do it! You say you can't stop dancing? Don't!! Enjoy!

You can use it like the first form and ask questions to get your day started, or you can do it to warm up your body for the day. Your movements may be very subtle one day and very wild the next. Experiment and begin to sense the energies around you and how you move with them.

Please remember these forms are just a place to start. When you get used to the energies and how you interact with them you will discover a form and feel that is entirely your own.

The Tool

Personal Experiences With The Tool

The following stories are included to give the reader an idea of some of the experiences we have had with The Tool. We hope they bring a little more clarity to the process and encourage you to, as Carolyn would say, "Just Do It." Enjoy.

CAROL

Being a workaholic was my way of life, or I should say my way of avoiding life. Who could fault me for not dealing with life if I was working? Even if I had wanted to use The Tool (which I didn't), I kept myself too busy. For the next eighteen months I bought into that "too busy" mis-perception even as I watched others around me practicing the darn Tool, getting answers, making gentle changes, growing, expanding and having more fun.

The Tool

...so out of desperation and a sense of last resort, I started using The Tool

When I finally decided to try it, it was like, "O.K., I'll give it five minutes and see what happens." Focusing more on the time than anything, of course, I wasn't aware of anything happening. I held an absolute in my mind that it wouldn't work for me and I proved it.

Next thing I knew, I broke out with a case of whole body hives. I'd never had them before or since. As a result of the hives, I spent long periods of time soaking in baking soda baths which was the only natural relief I had from the itching.

Trapped in my tub, unable to keep busy with work or distractions, the thoughts flooding my mind were making me crazy, so out of desperation and a sense of last resort, I started using The Tool. And it worked! Not always quickly then, sometimes an "Aha!" showed up a couple of days or a week later, after I quit looking so hard for it. I felt a lot of emotions and did more than I thought was my share of crying without any conscious understanding of what it was about.

Gradually I began to understand the thoughts that controlled me and ran my life. I began to see my untruths, the parts I tried to hide not only from others but from myself.

The Tool

This Tool, though simple, was not easy for me. For almost a year I thought I could only get answers while immersed in water.

Before learning The Tool my only motivating force was fear. Now I am able to motivate myself because I want to. Need and fear still show up regularly, but I'm able to recognize them along with the formerly paralyzing symptoms.

Using The Tool, I allow myself to see the truth with little or no judgment. I understand how my perceptions were appropriate when I was four years old, but not now. I understand how my thoughts protect me, and gain insight into other ways to protect myself until a time when I may no longer need the protection. I am now able to gain perspective, awareness and perceptions that were totally, consciously unknown to me before I used The Tool.

One really big issue for me is risking. Actually it never was an issue before because I didn't risk. Lately I have been playing with risking from information received through The Tool. Basically, if something felt risky to me everyone who would have been involved became my mother, ready to swiftly and harshly punish me. It has been a long time since I surrounded myself with people like that but I kept on reacting as if nothing had changed.

I was in a habit of waking up every morning thinking I was the same as yesterday. As a result of checking in to discern the differences, I am frequently amazed and thrilled about exploring and discovering without an expectation of the outcome. Learning to detach from certain pictures and absolutes has improved my life tremendously.

At first I had to force myself to take risks. I would feel sick and think of all sorts of excuses not to risk. Using The Tool is not one of my favorite activities, yet time after time I would go back to it just to make sure. But after I took the steps, it was unbelievable. Every time I was pleased with the results. Enough times that I was really encouraged to continue both using The Tool and risking.

An important aspect of The Tool is to be clear about what we want. If confused, then use The Tool for clarity before asking for anything. More than a few times I manifested unpleasant things for myself only to recognize later that I got what I asked for when I was confused or didn't know what I was talking about.

Do the basic Tool until you get the hang of it, then create your own way if you want.

In the days when I thought prayer was the only way available, I thought I had to be very serious and very reverent. I tried to hide my fear or anger or anxiety from God just as I tried to hide them from everyone. I even prayed every day when I didn't want to, just so God wouldn't think I only contacted him when I needed something, and I always spoke in a sweet voice.

To me, the truly cool thing about the energies is that they are always there and they respond no matter what tone of voice I use, so I don't waste energy hiding. The energies are there for us to use or not. It is our choice. They don't even care if we only call when our backs are to the wall. Of course, experience has taught me if I check in with them periodically, I make wiser choices and decisions and my back doesn't feel that wall nearly as often as in times past.

The next day I took the riskiest risk of my life so far, and the relationship that had plagued me for months died right then and a new one was born— With the same man.

The Tool

Recently, I was in a lot of pain because of a relationship. Everywhere I looked I saw pain. I know if I am seeing pain I am looking in the wrong direction, but I couldn't seem to find a place to look that was away from the pain.

I was taking many steps to do things differently which resulted in pleasant feedback in other areas, but the relationship pain remained. Nothing appeared to work in that area. One day when I felt very frustrated and angry, I yelled (not out loud, just in my mind), "I don't know where to look! You guys show me where to look and I'll look there!"

Almost immediately events took place that looked like the relationship was over. Precisely the worst scenario for me. I felt forced to come to terms with letting go—giving him up. I cried and cried. I was miserable. I did The Tool all night and all the next day. I never did that before. I changed my mind dozens of times about what I would do.

The next day I took the riskiest risk of my life so far, and the relationship that had plagued me for months died right then and a new one was born— With the same man.

I have enjoyed aspects of relationships but never enjoyed a total relationship and realize now that I have never even been a participant in a total relationship before. We are having lots of fun with this one, really enjoying it.

I am actively participating now, while I formerly waited to see what the other person did before I took a step in any direction. I intentionally take risks, intentionally explore and discover. I stick around when situations arise that I used to run from. It is scary because of the "unknown" factor. It is uncomfortable for the same reason, but each time I stay and explore, I discover another aspect of us that I like, another reason to explore further. I am beginning to understand what it means to thrive rather than exist.

CAROLYN

I was first introduced to the idea of active introspection with a short written instruction sheet and a copy of a long audio tape from which the guided instructions were derived. Something for both the visually and the auditorily oriented personality, so it was pre-

The Tool

sumably simple; read the instructions through, put on the tape and *Just Do It,* yes? No.

I knew about chakras. I didn't know they all had names, but I had heard of them. For a while even, I had done a form of chakra contemplation from Ken Keyes' *Handbook to a Higher Consciousness*, but that was when chakras had numbers instead of names. I already knew how to count to seven so that was no problem. And Ram Dass had taught a chakra meditation in which he encouraged starting at the heart level and going up, ignoring the lower ones. Perhaps on the theory that we were already immersed enough in worldly matters. Also I had done transcendental Meditation, TM, for several years. TM was not one of those empty the mind techniques, but it wasn't active either. In TM you just put the key in the ignition (sat down), started the motor (began repeating a mantra), and let it idle for twenty minutes taking whatever came and doing absolutely nothing with it. With all that experience why should I have anticipated that I might have difficulty learning a new technique?

What struck me immediately about this active introspection was how busy it was. First I had to decide on an issue to put to Allowance and then remember that it was Allowance I was talking to. Then I had to address Allegiance about the steps to get to wherever it was I wanted to go, and Will and Power for an effective way to put the steps into effect. Then Love..well you get the picture. There was a lot to remember: the answer I had gotten to my previous question and who had given me that answer, who I was to talk to next and why, and what was I going to do with that next bit of information. Then when I got all the way up to the top, hopefully without skipping anyone, or calling anyone by the wrong name, or asking anyone an inappropriate question, I didn't get to *Just Do It,* I had to start the whole process over again and refine it. And then refine it again.

It was frustrating. I would get up to Wisdom and not remember what Harmony had said or whether I had even remembered to talk to Harmony. Or I would get to Knowledge and be sure I must have skipped Love. Should I go back to Love and start over from there? Or go back to Love and then return to Knowledge? What if I went back to Love on the chance I had skipped it but really I hadn't? That would mean I had doubled up on Love, so then would I be out of balance with the rest?

Like many others, I have come from an "If you can't do it right, don't do it" conditioning. It was liberating to discover that, while it is possible not to do it, it is not possible to do it wrong. Just Do It.

The Tool

And if I inadvertently skipped one without realizing it, would I be out of balance without knowing it and would that invalidate the answers I was getting? You can see I took this very seriously.

Actually I took it so seriously that I decided I couldn't possibly do it right, so I might as well postpone doing it until some time in the future when I could get a better grasp of it. Perhaps in another lifetime. This attitude prevailed for quite a while until I began to observe that the people I knew who were actually *Just Doing It* seemed to be getting things together in a most remarkable fashion. They appeared to be involved with and directing their own lives with immense enjoyment, as if life was for active participation and not a spectator sport.

This gave me something to beat myself up about, especially after I finally began hearing what I had been told from the beginning, that you can't do it wrong except by *Just Not Doing It.* I could see that if I had continued to *Just Do It* from the time I started I would, with practice, have long since learned to do it as easily and automatically as I drive a car.

My solution was, if I can't do it wrong *I'll Do It My Way* until I get the hang of it. I started by simply "breathing into the chakras." I would do this perhaps two or three times a day. Usually I would start with two breaths or three in each one, but if I felt scattered I might go through the chakras several times, breathing only once or twice in each one until I felt calm and comfortable enough to spend a more extended time with each one. Eventually I had spent enough time getting acquainted with each chakra and its energy so that I was then comfortable doing the process as prescribed, asking the questions and clarifying the answers. Sometimes I confine myself to the focused breathing and then write in a journal. Often answers come to me as I write. Sometimes answers come to me outside the process as soon as I have asked myself a question.

Like many others, I have come from an "If you can't do it right, don't do it" conditioning. It was liberating to discover that, while it is possible not to do it, it is not possible to do it wrong. *Just Do It.*

GWEN

My internally-developed 'life message' was that anything new was going to be painful and difficult, that, of course, I would feel like a failure, and that others would be able to master whatever it was with relative ease. Those unspoken, and almost unconscious, rules established, I approached The Tool with an unrealistic amount of fear. I had been successful, in the past, with various forms of meditations that had temporarily relieved me from my consistent internal attacks. But confronting my internal dialogue, with the intent of changing the way that I saw myself or others, was not really a perspective I had ever even considered.

This said, you can imagine how thrilled I was at the prospect of confronting some of my beliefs, attitudes, and habits *by myself*. Instead of ignoring them completely, hoping they would go away, dumping them on someone around me, or finding another book, person, or rule that would fix them for me. What do you mean, I didn't want to change? Of course, I did: I wanted to move to another planet that would fit my picture of my self! What do you mean I was unwilling to cooperate? Of course I was, if there was any chance I could get someone to agree with me.

So much for realism. I enjoyed the unconscious notion that I was right, at all costs, and that anything external to me—that didn't agree with me—was simply ignorant of my own personal experience, emotions, and decisions. In other words, everyone different was either bad or wrong! (And probably some other things besides, which I won't mention here.)

Okay, so on to The Tool. (What do you mean, my personal history sounds somewhat mundane? I'm not defensive. I agree!)

It felt kind of good to breathe to the Energies, despite the persistent feeling that I was doing it wrong. Even with my fear, this was a new place to explore, and I did have the idea that I would find something new. Maybe something exciting; maybe something that would prove to me I was okay. I think, more than anything else, that I desperately wanted something, or someone, to assure me that I was not bad; that my life wasn't so wrong; that maybe I was not the horrible person I believed myself to be. Maybe, after so many efforts and failures with everything and everyone else,

The Tool

this—whatever it was—would actually help me to change. At least, there was hope.

I don't remember everything; it's been seven years. But I do remember feeling—well, sort of comforted. Having someone, or something, to talk to. And I remember that it took a while before anything really seemed to happen. I don't think I experienced much at first, so I just kept on trying. Finally, I seemed to hear something—a feeling, a voice—telling me something. This was encouraging, but when I found out that Carol saw colors, I became terribly discouraged again. Oh darn, why couldn't I get it right? Why couldn't I see colors? But it was still the best (meaning only) answer I had, so I just kept plodding along with a fair amount of consistency. At first, it took me a long time—an hour sometimes, sometimes more.

I find it difficult to share this next part with you, because you might see it as something other than just my experience, and stop using The Tool before you start. But I know that everyone is different, so I get to trust that you will choose whatever will benefit you the most. Just don't judge yourself to be like me!

The Tool

Here goes: I had an extra room at the back of my house, breezy and sparsely furnished, small and bright, with vine-covered windows, close to the trees. I called it my 'yoga room' because I could do my yoga there, undressed and in privacy, and also meditate whenever I wanted. Well, this room became my 'confrontation room', because I had never confronted and resolved my issues with myself in my entire life—and I had tons of them.

In this room, I used The Tool to confront everything I had never liked about me, or the way I had treated others, or the way that others had treated me. In other words, this room became MY BIG EMOTION ROOM. Many times I would spend entire Saturdays in this room, working with The Tool. I would question The Energies, write down the answers, and question some more. I would let myself cry, or scream, or breathe, or do whatever I felt like doing. I would emerge from the room pale but somehow victorious: Once again, *I had faced my own emotions and survived!* In time, I would expand my idea of self-worth to more interaction with others, but at the time, this Tool was all I had.

Others seem to notice the changes in me more than I do. I just notice how much easier life is for me, how much more I enjoy being around people (more than I ever thought I could), and that I see things differently.

The Tool

I would not necessarily recommend that anyone else use The Tool as I did. It worked for me, because I was isolated and very stuck, and because I truly felt that I could trust no one. I saw an opportunity for self-therapy, and I used it ruthlessly on myself. But The Tool is a gentle form of self-questioning; no one would have to use it to tear away at their identity in the way that I did. On the other hand, the self-Knowledge I gained in this persistent way was priceless to me. It gave me momentum to continue.

Eventually, I found these self-confronting sessions valuable in other ways. My son moved back into my life and we experienced the joy of mending our relationship together. In more ways than one, I began to find the parts of me that had been lost. I started to see that I hadn't been lost, just disconnected from parts of my self. The contemplation began to reveal those lost parts to me.

Another wonderful, unexpected thing happened: I actually began to share parts of The Tool that I had experienced with others. I, who was so convinced that I had little to give (the 'little' was actually 'little willingness'). Carol and I were at a retreat - Carol was always so open with me that I felt free to talk with her. Anyway, she was experiencing pain in her stomach. I suggested that she "Talk to the little girl whose feelings were in there," and to ask that child what those feelings were. I confided what the little child in me had said to me, and she said, "Oh, Gwen, that's beautiful! Would you write that down for me?" I was amazed because she saw colors and I couldn't, so I thought that she could do this Tool better. (No, I have never been insecure or competitive, as you can see.) Anyway, I wrote it down and others have found it useful. This tells me that any of our experiences—no matter how we see them—can be gifts to others. Simply knowing that has changed me.

So how am I today? (Perfect, sure.) Actually, I don't worry about myself as much as I used to. Others seem to notice the changes in me more than I do. I just notice how much easier life is for me, how much more I enjoy being around people (more than I ever thought I could), and that I see things differently. Differently how? How different? I am not sure—but there seems to be more in each day to live, and less in each day that I have to prove. For me, that is definitely progress.

The Tool

Also, of course, there are my Friends: The Friends I have found in The Tool. I know that because they are there, because I can confide in them, because they create with me and through me, because I can always turn to them and put my internal house in order—because of all that, I can finally be Home. Home in my self; Home on the Earth; Home with those around me. Because of them, I am no longer looking for my Home.

Part 4

Your Chapter

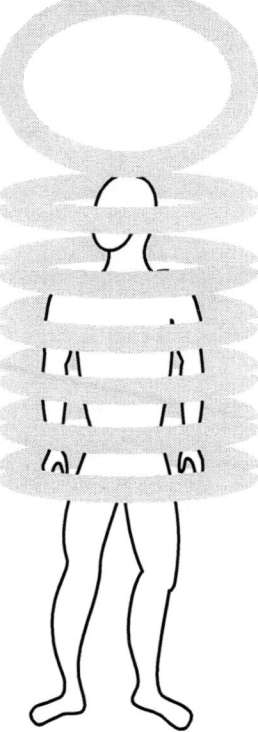

The Tool

When you find a situation that you keep reacting to, remember this chapter as the place you can write down your reactions and discover the truth of those reactions.

Your Chapter

In this last, unwritten chapter, it is the hope that you will begin to write the story of your life. Perhaps not the story you are used to telling yourself and others; and not the story of who you are based on what you do, but the story of your life based on who you are. We as human beings are so much larger than the simple labels we give ourselves. We are emotional beings. We are the fears and joys, the hopes and despairs and the dreams and the doubts of our lives. This story is not meant to be told to the world, but only to your Self. The Self that waits patiently for the truth.

Treat this chapter as a place you can be totally honest with yourself. When you find a situation that you keep reacting to, remember this chapter as the place you can write down your reactions and as the place you can discover the truth of those reactions. Trust that the truth can help give you the strength to change. As you write this chapter see if your life doesn't begin to

The Tool

change as well. Welcome that change and use it to grow and expand from the person you think you should be into the person you want to be.

There are a couple of sections. The first is simply designed to present a visual way to see the flow of the energies and to have a place to write down your answers. For some people this is a great way to do the process, while for others it may not be appropriate. Try it and see what works the best for you.

It is important to remember, and it bears repeating, that your answers are yours alone and they will be unique to you. If the form of the questions given here doesn't work for you then use a form that does. This doesn't mean to skip parts because they are uncomfortable, it means to find a way that gets you through the entire process in a consistent manner. That consistency will build a foundation and a consistent way to look at life.

The first step is to identify the problem, fear or anger or anything that you want to change. Identifying the real issue can sometimes be the most difficult thing of all. If you are having trouble with this part, then it may be a great place to start with The Tool. Perhaps, "What is the real issue?" would be a great question.

Let Allowance set the focus for you. Its job is to narrow your view into the place that is giving you the trouble. *Allow* that to happen. If you are having trouble getting the 'right' answers, remember that focus from Allowance, and design your questions around getting the right answers. Don't forget that you can 'make up' answers as well, because they will most likely come from the process anyway.

You will notice two parts to the questions in Allowance. One part is designed to address a fear and the other is designed to address a desire. You will know which part you are working with.

The Tool evolves and changes with each round of questions and with each new day and challenge. This ever-changing nature of The Tool does not lend itself very well to the strict form of the questions that follow in this section. So be sure and remember the *intent* of each question. That means to ask Allegiance a 'steps' related question, W & P a 'control and cooperation' question etc. Visit each energy and let the process flow.

We have included space to do the process three times and it is recommended that you do it all three times if you can keep focused. As you practice you may find yourself getting to answers in a shorter period but to build a firm foundation, try it three times.

We have the standard copyright paragraph in the beginning of the book which forbids copying things out of this book, but please feel free to copy the workbook section if it will help you to practice the process.

So, the first step — What's bugging you?

Write down the thing that is causing fear or anxiety or pain in your life. This is the focus for this round of questions.

_____

_____

_____

_____

_____

_____

Step 1. Allowance

Now place this fear or anger to Allowance to see it for the truth. You might say, "Allowance, why do I react to *that* the way I do? I want to change *this* aspect of myself." Keep the answer, no matter how crazy it sounds. And keep the focus for the round of questions.

_____

_____

_____

_____

_____

_____

_____

_____

Now look at the answer Allowance has given and see if there is another way that the fear may be served. You might ask, *"Allowance how does the fear serve me and what is another way it can be?"* This may look like a desire hidden within the fear. (There are a lot of examples of desires that are hidden within a fear. You may have the fear of being close to someone which is hiding your true desire to learn how to be close. Or a fear of success might be hiding a desire to view your life as a success. There's many more, but rather than list all the possibilities just keep the concept in mind.) If a desire does appear then perhaps ask, *"What is the purpose of this desire?"*

Step 2. Allegiance

Now take this purpose to Allegiance and see what steps there are to fulfilling this purpose. You might ask Allegiance:

"Allegiance, I have seen the purpose of my involvement, what steps are there for me to take in order for me to fulfill this purpose?"

_____

_____

_____

_____

_____

_____

_____

_____

Step 3. Will and Power

Now we want to find a way to control ourselves, and cooperate with ourselves and others in order for a change to happen.

Ask Will and Power, "How can I cooperate with myself and others and control myself towards this purpose?"

_____

_____

_____

_____

_____

_____

_____

_____

_____

Step 4. Love

Now ask Love to discern your involvement. "Am I close to this thing or far away? How will it benefit me to act in this new way?"

_____

_____

_____

_____

_____

_____

_____

_____

_____

5. Harmony

Now ask Harmony how to balance the energies to create the most harmoniously. "Is one of the energies needed more than another? Less?"

_____

_____

_____

_____

_____

_____

_____

_____

_____

Step 6. Knowledge

Knowledge, show me all the times in the past I have felt the same way in similar situations.

_____

_____

_____

_____

_____

_____

_____

_____

Take these experiences and breathe them in knowing they form a part of who you are. Now blow them away and understand that was yesterday and tomorrow can be different.

Step 7. Wisdom

Now ask Wisdom to show you a piece of the future. If it is fearful, ask to see the smaller fear that may be a part of this larger fear. If it is not fearful, then ask Wisdom to show you the benefit of the new action you want to take.

_____

_____

_____

_____

_____

_____

_____

_____

Place this answer back down to Allowance and begin again.

Allowance

"Allowance what is the truth of my fear? Show this to me without judgment. Or what is the purpose of my desire? How does it serve my life?"

_____

_____

_____

_____

_____

_____

_____

Now look at the truth of the fear and see if there is another way that the fear may be served. You might say, "Allowance how does the fear serve me and what is another way that it may?" This may look like a desire hidden within the fear. If it does then what is the purpose of the desire?

Allegiance

Now take this purpose to Allegiance and see what steps there are to fulfilling this purpose. You might ask Allegiance:

"Allegiance, I have seen the purpose of my involvement, what steps are there for me to take in order for me to fulfill this purpose."

_____

_____

_____

_____

_____

_____

_____

_____

Will and Power

Now we want to find a way to control ourselves and cooperate with ourselves and others in order for the creation to exist.

Ask Will and Power, "How can I cooperate with others and control myself towards this purpose?"

_____

_____

_____

_____

Love

Now ask Love to discern your involvement. "Am I close to this thing or far away? How will it benefit me to act in this new way?"

_____

_____

_____

Harmony

Now ask Harmony how to balance the energies to create the most harmoniously. Is one of the energies needed more than another? Less?

Knowledge

"Knowledge show me all the times in the past I have felt the same way in similar situations."

_____

_____

_____

_____

_____

_____

_____

Take these experiences and breathe them in knowing they form a part of who you are. Now blow them away and understand that was yesterday and tomorrow can be different.

Wisdom

Now ask Wisdom to show you a piece of the future. If it is fearful, ask to see the smaller fear that may be a part of this larger fear. If it is not, then ask Wisdom to show you the benefit of the new action you want to take.

_____

_____

_____

_____

Place this answer back down to Allowance and begin again

Allowance

"Allowance what is the truth of my fear? Show this to me without judgment." Or, "What is the purpose of my desire? How does it serve my life?"

_____

_____

_____

_____

Now look at the truth of the fear and see if there is another way that the fear may be served. You might say, "Allowance how does the fear serve me and what is another way that it may?" This may look like a desire hidden within the fear. If it does then what is the purpose of the desire?

Allegiance

Now take this purpose to Allegiance and see what steps there are to fulfilling this purpose. You might ask Allegiance: "Allegiance I have seen the purpose of my involvement, what steps are there for me to take in order for me to fulfill this purpose."

_____

_____

_____

_____

_____

_____

_____

Will and Power

Now ask to find a way to control yourself and cooperate with yourself and others in order for the creation to exist.

_____

_____

_____

Ask Will and Power, "How can I cooperate with others and control myself towards this purpose?"

_____

_____

_____

_____

_____

_____

Love

Now ask Love to discern your involvement. "Am I close to this thing or far away? How will it benefit me to act in this new way?"

_____

_____

_____

Harmony

Now ask Harmony how to balance the energies to create the most harmoniously. Is one of the energies needed more than another? Less?

_____

_____

_____

_____

_____

Knowledge

"Knowledge show me all the times in the past I have felt the same way in similar situations."

_____

_____

Take these experiences and breathe them in, knowing they form a part of who you are. Now blow them away and understand that was yesterday and tomorrow can be different.

Wisdom

Now ask Wisdom to show you a piece of the future. This third time through should show you a very excited place in Wisdom. Hang on to the excitement as long as you can.

_____

_____

_____

This is the place you might find yourself very far 'out'. If you are doing this in the evening you might want to fall asleep. Before you do, ask Wisdom to let you return to your body. Maybe using the *Long Breath* (see page 55), feel your toes, your ankles, your legs and every part of your body. Lastly, open your eyes, if you aren't asleep already; close them again and relax into a great night's sleep.

If it's not bedtime skip the 'close them again' part and have a great day.

Daily Energy Exercise

There are seven energies and coincidentally there are seven days of the week. Here is an exercise where you can try to get more familiar with the energies and how they affect your life. Simply assign one energy to each of the different days of the week.

It is probably not too important which day you assign to which energy but you might start with Allowance on Monday, Allegiance on Tuesday etc. Then on each day, focus your thoughts to the energy for that day. An important thing to remember is that each of these days represents only *one* energy, so the things that come up are not to be acted upon immediately, only contemplated and observed for the truth that they hold.

If you find an issue that is painful within any day, mark it down either in the space provided or in your mind, and use The Tool to help resolve the issue that evening.

Monday

Allowance

These are the things you will and will not Allow. This might start out with some angry issues, so be gentle with the things that come up. You might find yourself saying, "I will NOT ALLOW this thing or that." Remember this is only one energy and the things you will see are distorted by this narrow view. Observe your feelings for the purpose of learning about yourself.

This can also be a great day to get focused for the week. The things you will Allow are the things you focus your energy on. The things that you will not Allow are the things that do not get your attention. Purpose is also a great thought to connect with Allowance.

Monday's Observations

_____

_____

_____

_____

_____

Tuesday

Allegiance

Today can be spent with the thought of joining and of steps toward a purpose or desire. Watch for any steps that you see that are a response to an anger from Allowance. Again this is only a single energy and the steps might be inappropriate and out of balance.

Allegiance and Allowance form purpose together so it might be good to think about joining with a purpose.

Tuesday's Observations

_____

_____

_____

_____

_____

_____

Wednesday

Will and Power

Control. This can be a wild day because so much of our society is based in control and being controlled. Observe yourself and see where you sit. Do you like to control situations? Are you easily controlled? How can you control yourself instead of other people? Again, don't try to change too much too fast, just observe to learn more about who you are.

Wednesday's Observations

_____

_____

_____

_____

_____

_____

_____

Thursday

Love

Can you separate your Self from others? Are you too separate? Notice the similarities and the differences between you and your co-workers. We are all human, which is a great bonding thought, but look, we are all different in subtle ways. Discernment is the keyword for a day observing Love.

Thursday's Observations

Friday

Harmony

What's the big picture? Harmony can let you see things from more than one perspective. This might be a great day to put yourself in someone else's shoes. Is there someone that you have a hard time with? What must it be like from the place they are looking?

On this day you might think, "I could really use more self control," or "I'm always so judgmental." This is Harmony telling you to use more Will and Power and Allowance respectively.

Friday's Observations

_____

_____

_____

_____

_____

_____

Saturday

Knowledge
Knowledge wants to show you who you have been in the past. This can be tough if you are really judgmental, but you do get to look. Sometimes some buried things will surface on this day. If you can look at it with an eye that looks for the truth without judgment, then this can really be valuable.

I have had some tough Saturdays and then thought, "Oh yeah, no wonder this is a Knowledge day."

Saturday's Observations

___

___

___

___

___

___

Sunday

Wisdom

This is a great day for daydreaming and just hanging around. Have you ever noticed how hard it is to get anything done on a Sunday? Everyone's just hanging around dreaming about the future. You can too.

Be as unlimited as you can on this day. Get real wild and see what comes up. This is a great way to 'exercise' Wisdom.

Sunday's Observations

_____

_____

_____

_____

_____

_____

It is our sincere hope that the Tools and information we have presented is genuinely useful in your life, and that they bring to you a little more clarity and a little more joy throughout your day. If you have some especially wild adventures, or you would just like to share your experiences, you can write us at Balance Productions, P.O. Box 1681, Vista, Ca. 92085-1681. Enjoy.